Pursuing Gold

A HISTORY & CRITICAL THINKING
CURRICULUM

ENDORSEMENTS

The History and Critical Thinking Curriculum by Cynthia L. Simmons to accompany *Pursuing Gold* is a wonderful way to bring the family together around a good book. The guide asks key reading comprehension questions, offers wonderful historical insight into the setting and details of the book, and asks questions designed to challenge students to think deeply about historical and spiritual issues. It's a wonderful tool to help your family experience history and literature in a deeper way and is sure to spark some wonderful discussions!

—Bonnie Rose Hudson, director of SchoolhouseTeachers.com and author/publisher of WriteBonnieRose.com curriculum

This curriculum is rich with fun facts and information that is a wonderful addition to any homeschool curriculum. The vibrant photos, questions, and interactive exercises deliver the information in a fun way, making history a subject to look forward to!

—Michelle S. Lazurek, former homeschool mother, *Helping People Reach Their Potential.* Illumination 2016 Enduring Light Silver Medalist, author of *An Invitation To The Table: Embracing the Gift of Hospitality*

This curriculum combines history and critical thinking in a unique way, especially as an addition to an accurate historical fiction novel. I especially like how the author adds plenty of useful information throughout the curriculum. Great job!

—Jennifer Henn, author, *The Well-Adjusted Homeschooler*

What a fresh approach to history. Your child can learn about the history of the ink pen, stethoscope, Morse code, and other fascinating topics. I especially like the information on teaching kids to better handle their money. I recommend.

—Michael Anderson, former owner/operator of award-winning Christian bookstores and co-founder of the Christian Authors Guild, Inc.

Cynthia Simmons brings the history of money to life in her *Pursuing Gold* curriculum for tweens and teens. This course goes beyond historical fact by weaving the companion fiction book of the same title into the lessons. The student is able to critically apply the concepts gleaned from the material into everyday life while being captivated by the accompanying story. The activities and questions contained in each lesson will hold the child's attention and create an anticipation to know more. *Pursuing Gold* not only engages the brain but captures the imagination.

—**Lori Wildenberg**, co-founder of 1st Corinthians 13 Parenting ministry, national speaker, parent coach, and author of five parenting books including: *The Messy Life of Parenting: Powerful and Practical Ways to Strengthen Family Connections*.

Pursuing Gold

A HISTORY & CRITICAL THINKING
CURRICULUM

Cynthia L. Simmons

PUBLISHING THE POSITIVE

ELK LAKE PUBLISHING INC
Plymouth, Massachusetts

Copyright Notice

Pursuing Gold: A History/Critical Thinking Curriculum

Cover and Interior Design: Derinda Babcock
Editor(s): Susan K. Stewart, Deb Haggerty
Author Represented By: WordWise Media Services

PUBLISHED BY: Elk Lake Publishing, Inc., 35 Dogwood Drive, Plymouth, MA 02360, 2019

Library Cataloging Data

Names: Simmons, Cynthia L. (Cynthia L. Simmons)
Pursuing Gold: A History/Critical Thinking Curriculum / Cynthia Simmons
144 p. 280 mm × 216 mm (8.5 in x 11 in.)
Description: Curriculum designed to accompany the book *Pursuing Gold: A Novel of the Civil War.*
Identifiers: ISBN-13: 978-1-950051-46-5 (trade) | 978-1-950051-47-2 (POD)
Key Words: Civil War, Confederacy, Chattanooga, Rebels, Gold as Currency, Banking, Customs of the 1860s
LCCN: 2019937784 Nonfiction

DEDICATION

To all those who homeschool their children. You deserve great applause for your dedication to your children's educations.

ACKNOWLEDGMENTS

I must thank Mavian Arocha-Rowe a thousand times for her editing and constant help.

Thanks to the staff at Elk Lake, Deb Haggerty, Derinda Babcock, and Susan K. Stewart, for all their efforts.

INTRODUCTION

You may wonder why I wrote this book, and I might too when I get bogged down halfway through. (I hope that made you smile.) I have several reasons but let me start by saying I have raised five children, educating them at home. My youngest had significant learning challenges, and I acquired information and experience over the years that I am anxious to pass along. I Timothy encourages the older women to teach the younger how to love their husbands and children, and I am thrilled to offer you some of what I acquired during those busy years. As part of the church, we should be obsessed with impacting the next generation so we can pass along our faith.

It's my privilege to help you. I did extensive research into the finances of the Civil War, and why should excellent information go to waste? I am offering a history/literature/critical thinking curriculum to enhance your school or homeschool by offering information you might not find elsewhere, and I added photos and activities. As a retired RN, I have insights into medicine of the 18th century and the ways the body responds to treatments. You may use some or all of my activities at your discretion. Homeschool moms, remember those younger ones will pick up a lot as they watch and listen, so include them in the warmth as you study. I wanted to implant a love of learning, and I hope your kids catch that too.

Additional material to teach about money and budgeting and about critical thinking is included in the appendices.

—Cynthia L Simmons

"You shall teach [God's truths] them diligently to your children, and shall talk of them when you sit in your house, when you walk by the way, when you lie down and when you rise up" (Deut. 6:7 NKJV).

CHAPTER 1

Money has not always been green paper or plastic credit cards. In the 1860s when the Civil War started in the United States, people used coins for money because the coin had value; i.e., either gold or silver or nickel. Paper was too easy to fake, and no one wanted counterfeit money. Wars tend to put stress on a nation's economy because the government has to spend extra money on war supplies and ammunition. During the Civil war, both the Union and Confederacy switched to paper money.

The Confederacy chose to accept loans rather than rely only on taxes to raise money. Early in 1861, they offered bonds with interest to raise money and received gifts to cover expenses. And they seized gold from Union properties they took over. They never passed a legal tender law, but they didn't have gold, so they offered paper bills to cover debts. Big banks loaned their gold and silver to the government and began printing money from their bank. If the Confederacy had won, the banks would have been fine because the government would have owed them money. However, after the Confederates lost the war their paper money was worthless, and banks that loaned them money died.

In 1862, the North passed a legal tender law, which meant the government proclaimed the green paper as appropriate for paying debts. They chose to make the paper green because that color would be harder to copy

A photo of a Confederate bill. The size and shapes of bills varied since different banks published them. Note this one is for twenty-five cents.

Questions:

1. What did Peter mean when he said C&R Bank was fully invested in the community?
2. Peter wanted bank dealings to be legal and fair. What type of man was he?
3. What is a rumor? Why would that frighten Mary Beth?
4. People did not have telephones in the 1860s. They sent messages by telegraph or mail instead. Look on the internet to see who invented telephones.
5. What is the role of a spy? Could a Christian be a spy? Read Joshua 2.
6. Why was Chattanooga valuable to the Union?
7. "I wished I'm a never" was a saying common among country folk. What do you think it means?

Cynthia L. Simmons

Use these words: invest, legal, rumor, dilemma, missive, austerity, appease

Across
2. obey the law
5. calm someone's anger
7. cut back on spending

Down
1. problem
3. put money in a business with hopes of profit later
4. letter

Name

Chapter 1 Crossword Puzzle

CHAPTER 2

Medical care in the 1860s was much different than today. Doctors usually made house visits even though they had an office. They carried a black bag called a Gladstone bag that contained equipment to diagnose and treat almost any medical problem. Doctors even had materials to perform surgery, if necessary. Here are a few things they would have: thermometer, syringes, scalpel, tweezers, stethoscope, tourniquet, bandages, suture supplies, and herbal remedies.

Doctors did not understand the causes of disease, and some of their treatments seem barbaric. They attempted to remove inflammation with plasters or bleeding. If someone was flushed and running a temperature, bleeding would reduce the temperature and redness. However, such treatment could weaken the person and make them unable to throw off the infection.

At the time, most people cared for their family at home. Wounded soldiers came to Chattanooga when Nashville fell to the Union in 1862. The residents converted a warehouse into a hospital, which the military ran. They called it Newsome Hospital.

1. Based on what you see in the story, what do you think "lying abed" means?
2. Define prognosis.
3. Mr. Roper defined what a bank does. Write a summary of what he said. Why might a bank be important to the community?
4. What is a commodity?
5. What was a blockade?
6. What did a blockade runner do?
7. What is a munitions factory and why would Peter hesitate to invest?
8. Describe how you'd feel if you were stunned.
9. What did Eddie do that Mary Beth hated?

CHAPTER 3

1. What do you think of Anna Chandler's plan?
2. You'll note that Mrs. Chandler refers to Ellen as Mrs. Reverend McCallie. That was common at the time. Why do you think they did that?
3. What did courtship mean in the 1860s?
4. Did it differ from today's dating? How?
5. Why would banking involve interacting with customers?
6. What is foreshadowing? Give an example of foreshadowing in this chapter.
7. Define trepidation.
8. What kind of man is Lieutenant McDonald? How do you know?
9. "Take the air" was another expression used at the time. What do you think it means?

Use these words: prospectus, courtship, trepidation, dossier, commodities, munitions, blockade, prognosis, prudence.

<u>Across</u>
1. wisdom
6. romantic relationship prior to marriage
7. documents on a business
8. bullets and machines used in war

<u>Down</u>
2. raw material people need
3. fear
4. prevent a harbor from receiving goods
5. long-term outcome

Name

_____

Chapter 3 Crossword Puzzle

CHAPTER 4

Samuel Morse patented a machine called a telegraph, which transmitted sounds using Morse code by means of electrical wire. On the other end of the wire, a decoding machine printed out the sounds on a narrow sheet of paper, which people transcribed. In 1844, Morse demonstrated his new invention to Congress by transmitting the message "What God hath wrought." This new method of communication was widely used by the time of the Civil War.

1. Define dallied.
2. What do you think of Ruth? Why?
3. If you were Mrs. Chandler how would you feel about an army targeting your town?
4. What impact did the telegraph have on communication?
5. What was the General? What happened to it?
6. Describe Mr. Henderson.
7. What is a clash of arms?

Morse code used a series of short and long sounds to spell out words.

American Morse Code

A	▪ ▬	N	▬ ▪	1	▪ ▬ ▬ ▪
B	▬ ▪ ▪ ▪	O	▪ ▪	2	▪ ▪ ▬ ▪ ▪
C	▪ ▪ ▪	P	▪ ▪ ▪ ▪ ▪	3	▪ ▪ ▪ ▬ ▪
D	▬ ▪ ▪	Q	▪ ▪ ▬ ▪	4	▪ ▪ ▪ ▪ ▬
E	▪	R	▪ ▪ ▪	5	▬ ▬ ▬
F	▪ ▬ ▪	S	▪ ▪ ▪	6	▪ ▪ ▪ ▪ ▪ ▪
G	▬ ▬ ▪	T	▬	7	▬ ▬ ▪ ▪
H	▪ ▪ ▪ ▪	U	▪ ▪ ▬	8	▬ ▪ ▪ ▪ ▪
I	▪ ▪	V	▪ ▪ ▪ ▬	9	▬ ▪ ▪ ▬
J	▬ ▬ ▬ ▪	W	▪ ▬ ▬	0	▬▬▬
K	▬ ▪ ▬	X	▪ ▬ ▪ ▪	&	▪ ▪ ▪ ▪
L	▬	Y	▪ ▪ ▪ ▪	.	▪ ▪ ▪ ▪ ▪ ▪ ▪
M	▬ ▬	Z	▪ ▪ ▪ ▪	,	▪ ▬ ▪ ▬

Using the chart above, write out these messages in Morse code. Or if you are really ambitious, make a buzzing sound with your mouth and see if your friends can decode the words you buzz.

1. I have cake.
2. The party is tomorrow
3. We won the battle.
4. I got a new puppy.

Telegraph lines ran along railroad lines, as you can see in the photo below.

CHAPTER 5

Doctors in the 1860s had a tendency to make their patients stay in bed. However, we now understand extended bedrest harms the body. The bones lose their calcium, the muscles atrophy, the skin breaks down, and the patient is more prone to pneumonia and bladder infections. Our lungs and muscles need fresh air, and exercise is great for that. Plus, recent studies show exercise grows new brain cells and boosts our immune system.

Good Posture and Soldiers: A soldier had to stand up straight and tall when his superiors shouted, "Attention!" Practice standing with shoulders back and arms by your sides while keeping your knees loose. If you keep your tummy tight, it helps with balance. Your teacher can call you to attention when it's time for a break. Be prepared to stand tall with your arms by your sides. Soldiers always answer, "Sir, yes, sir!"

Saluting: Saluting started about the time of the Romans. Officials worried about being assassinated, so they required those who approached to raise their right hand to prove they meant no harm. A knight would raise his face mask to expose himself. Later, men would tap their hat and bow. This action evolved into touching the hat or raising it. Today, our military places a flat hand on their brow to acknowledge an officer. The British navy requires the one saluting show the open palm, however, because sailors often have dirty hands, our military chose a palm down salute.

1. Why didn't Mr. Nelson want Elsie in his store? Compare that attitude to Gal 3:28.
2. What reason did Mr. Roper give for Mary Beth visiting the grocer? How does that explain what a banker does?
3. What two types of discrimination do we see in this chapter?
4. Why doesn't God grant everything we pray for? See Isaiah 55:8-9
5. Mary Beth describes the problem of pain. If we believe God is good and all-powerful, why does he allow pain and suffering? Read Rom. 1: 18-32, and 8:28.

CHAPTER 6

God warned Adam and Eve they would die if they ate of the Tree of Knowledge of Good and Evil. The Bible teaches they died spiritually when they sinned and died physically later. Because of their choice, all of us face physical death, and death is serious business. Hebrews 9:27 says, "it is appointed for man to die once, and after that comes judgment." However, we do not have to fear death if we trust Jesus as our Savior.

"O death, where is your victory? O death, where is your sting? The sting of death is sin, and the power of sin is the law. But thanks be to God, who gives us the victory through our Lord Jesus Christ." I Cor. 15:55–57

Historical background

In the 1860s, there were fewer hospitals, and medical care had significant limitations. It wasn't uncommon for people to ask carefully after your health and that of your family because if you fell ill, you could die.

1. Dr. Smith tells Mary Beth her father is dying. Have you ever had someone close to you die? How did you feel?
2. Compare Mary Beth and Angela Phipps. Who do you like the best?
3. What do you think of Gustav Sadler? What is the basis of your opinion?
4. What do you think of how Peter handled Sadler? Look at Matt. 5:23- 25, Gal. 6:1, Matt. 18:15
5. Compare McDonald and Peter. Who do you like best?

CHAPTER 7

Mr. Roper suffered from congestive heart failure, which often comes from a lifetime of overwork, a high-fat diet, and/or high blood pressure. The heart becomes large and less efficient. Doctors medicate it with digitalis, which slows and strengthens the heart. Digitalis is a naturally occurring chemical found in foxglove, lily of the valley, the oleander tree, the strophanthrus vine, Kalanchoe, milkweed, and pheasant's eye. Today, pharmacists extract the chemicals in a lab where they can determine the strength and dosage. In the story, Mary Beth crushes and uses lily of the valley in a preparation for her father. Any of these plants can be dangerous to ingest, so keep them away from young children and pets. Eating them can cause cardiac failure.

Lily of the Valley. The flowers bloom in the spring, but the leaves, roots, stems, and flowers are all deadly.

Activity: Mint tea:

Fresh mint

Tea kettle

Water

Sugar

Teacup

Purchase fresh mint at a garden shop. Pick several leaves and wash them. Bring water to a rolling boil and pour over the leaves. After steeping four minutes, remove the leaves, add sugar, and enjoy.

Questions

1. What do Elsie's actions tell you about her?

2. Peter noted that everyone seemed to want the bank's money. Look up I Timothy 6:10 and James 4:3. Tell why that's true.

3. Why was Mary Beth angry with Peter when she found him talking to her father?

4. What risk did Peter take when he asked Mary Beth to consider courting him again? Would you have done what he did?

5. Why did Mary Beth respect Peter after he warned her about McDonald?

CHAPTER 8

Mary Beth worked hard in her herbal garden as this chapter opened. Herbs have been the basis for medicine for thousands of years. Some preparations like willow bark, the source of aspirin, and digitalis, which comes primarily from foxglove, have made a huge difference in Western medicine.

Today, however, a wise person will investigate scientific claims before using an over-the-counter treatment. That does not include testimonials where people claim to have improved. In a scientific test, a researcher limits anything that might change the results, has a control group, and takes careful note of the results. They will list objective symptoms rather than a vague claim someone may have of improved health.

I once read research about a person who claimed to have an ailment and visited numerous health food stores. He received all kinds of advice about the amount of herb he needed, from minute doses to very large. The wisest plan is to see a doctor who can help you with proper herbs/dosage. The FDA regulates herbal preparations as supplements, and they will investigate claims sellers make. Beware!

ACTIVITY: MAKE AN HERB GARDEN

Plan on a spot that receives about six hours of direct sun. Four hours of sun will work but check the plants you buy to make sure they can handle less sun. Next consider the soil. If there's a spot in the yard that gets sun and has rich dirt, that's perfect. The dirt should be worked until it's fine—without clumps, rocks, or roots. If you are a beginning gardener, you might want to do a raised bed by making a wood frame to fill with potting soil. Or you can use containers filled with soil like Miracle Gro.

Once the soil is ready, plant the seeds or purchase small seedlings. If you plant seedlings, be sure you dig a hole deep large enough to get the plants as deeply in the dirt as they were in the pot. Seeds take longer, but they work too. Next, dig a hole, and then fill it with water before placing the plant in the dirt.

Be sure you water regularly so the plants don't completely dry out, and do cuttings regularly. Herbs actually enjoy being cut back, and they reward you with fuller growth.

Questions:

1. You'll notice Mary Beth weeding. Read Genesis 3:18 and explain why we have weeds.

2. How did Mary Beth know Ruth had something on her mind?

3. What signals did Mr. Grant give that he was tense?

4. How dangerous would it be for Mr. Sadler to challenge Peter?

CHAPTER 9

As the chapter opens, notice Peter and Mary Beth walking on a wooden sidewalk toward the cafe. At that time, a city had roads of dirt. Buildings along the road would have a place to tie the horse and a wooden sidewalk, much like in some of the western movies you may have seen. A flat dirt road became a mess in the rain as water pooled. Engineers learned to build roads with the center higher than the sides, so the water would drain into gutters.

1. Fill in the blank using these words: infatuation, erupt, assignation, whim, scenario, pontificating
   A person who keeps talking so much you are annoyed is

   _____
   Another name for a date is _____
   _____ means a sudden gush.
   A sudden, crazy thought is a _____
   Feeling you might be in love is _____

2. Contrast Peter and Mary Beth's play.
3. When Mary Beth found her father in bed with bank papers, she tried to remove them, but he insisted on keeping them. Tell how this illustrates a woman's thoughts are different or the same as a man's.
4. At the end of the chapter, Mary Beth questions McDonald to learn more about him. What was his reaction? What does this tell you about him?
5. Sadler came to the Roper home and warned Mary Beth about Peter. How would you feel if someone talked negatively about someone you were beginning to love?

CHAPTER 10

In this chapter, note the oil lamp Peter used after dark. For years, people used either candles or oil lamps for light at night. Many farmers would rise and retire with the sun. Having electric lights allows us to stay up later; however, the artificial light can interfere with sleep. Our bodies produce melatonin as darkness falls. Keeping on lights means we might not produce enough to get sleepy. It's wise to turn off lights in the house to help you get sleepy at bedtime. Some people watch TV until they fall asleep, but the light from the TV can interfere with normal sleep cycles. To have a normal sleep cycle, plan on going to bed at the same time each night and turn down lights to prepare your body for sleep. Sit down just before bedtime, read a boring book, and you'll be surprised how fast you fall asleep.

The big crisis begins in this chapter when Mary Beth discovers a counterfeit bill with Peter's signature. At the time, large banks had loaned the Confederacy money and printed paper money in order to continue their normal transactions. The bills usually said they were worth gold and could be exchanged for gold. However, Peter and Mary Beth stayed on the gold standard since they feared the Confederacy would fall. If a crowd mobbed their bank wanting gold, they could lose the bank.

1. Mary Beth goes to Peter and reports Sadler doesn't respect Peter's abilities. If you had been Peter, what would you have done?
2. In the 1860s, people used coins of gold or silver, sometimes nickel. People valued those metals. What do you think of the way Sadler handled the situation?
3. How would you feel if you were Mary Beth and found money counterfeited with your bank's name?
4. Describe the problem Mrs. Chandler had with Ruth.
5. Mrs. Chandler wants to solve Peter's problems. How much should she be involved?

CHAPTER 11

You'll see Peter and his family traveling in a train in this chapter, and it's helpful to understand the background of the railway at the time. Because the North had a lot more industry, they had a larger network of trains, and the tracks were safer. The South was rural and had fewer tracks. In many cases, the railroad hired inexperienced people to build the Southern railways. So sometimes, the ties broke loose as the train passed over, causing wrecks, and killing travelers.

In theory, the steam locomotive could go much faster than a horse. However, the train stopped at every station along the way, which prolonged travel times. Express trains went at night, and they avoided the smaller stations. If locomotives could have gone at thirty miles per hour, the trip would have been much shorter.

SAFE FROM THE 1800s

1. Power of Attorney (POA) means you give someone permission to sign your name. Peter gave Mary Beth the ability to sign his name on bank documents while he was gone. How would you feel if someone gave you that permission?

2. Mary Beth discovers her housekeeper, Maud, has left without giving notice. Giving notice means you tell your employer you plan to stop working for him. Why do you think employers want notice?

3. Note that the Roper's hired their servants. How is that different than a slave?

4. What example do we have in Philemon regarding slaves and owners?

5. Mary Beth battles the problem of pain, as C.S. Lewis put it, "Only Christians have the problem. We have a holy, all powerful God, and yet he doesn't prevent suffering." In this chapter, she wonders if she should pray at all because God doesn't seem to answer. What would you tell her?

6. Ruth pretends to be asleep because she doesn't want to be in Savannah. What do you think of such a tactic?

CHAPTER 12

We are accustomed to email, which is delivered via computer and is faster than the post office 'snail mail.' However, in the early days, people picked up their mail at the post office. A stamp paid for delivery to your post office, not your home, unless you paid extra. In 1863, Congress passed a law making delivery to the home free if the city brought in enough income to cover the cost of delivery. From that time forward, people who used the post office had to put their street address on the envelope for delivery to their home. Of course, this wouldn't have affected states in the Confederacy. So, Mary Beth would have had to continue picking up her mail until after the war.

Fill in the blank with the correct word: mimic, prospectus, lucrative, detest, dividends
1. If you hate something, you _____ it.
2. When you want to borrow money, you write up a _____ to convince the bank you can pay them back.
3. A business pays _____ to investors.
4. You _____ when you pretend to be someone else.

CHAPTER 13

In this chapter, Mary Beth begins investigating her boarders' rooms and feels uncomfortable snooping. Her feelings came from her belief in personal property, which is taught in the Bible. She didn't ask to look through their things because she was looking for clues the way a detective would. When God forbade people to steal in the Ten Commandments, he was establishing that people have a right to own their possessions. This is a very important concept in our society and is opposite of the communist system. We do not hold all things in common. When everyone owns something, no one takes care of it. Many Old Testament laws regulated what happened when someone borrowed property and damaged or destroyed it. And many of our laws in this country are based on the right of personal property.

HISTORY OF THE INK PEN

You will notice Mr. Fields gave Peter a rather unique pen to sign documents. In the 1800s, it was common to use a quill (basically a feather) that had been trimmed for writing. The quill gave way to a pen with a steel or gold nib, which was dipped in ink. Obviously, you can't write much, so people kept an ink stand on their desk. Once they finished composing their letter, they would blot the page to soak up excess ink.

About the mid-1800s, inventors were working on a way to make a pen that held its own ink. It was tricky to make the ink flow smoothly and not leave nasty blotches of ink. John Jacob Parker patented a self-filling pen in 1813. Later, a Canadian druggist, Duncan MacKinnon, made a pen he called an "ink pencil." He gave one to Alonzo Cross, who fixed one flaw, and then created his own pen. Cross called his a stylographic pen and patented it in 1877. L.E. Waterman got upset with a pen that leaked and ruined a document. He set out to find a way to make a writing instrument that was easier to use. He patented one in 1888, but it wasn't until 1940 that the ballpoint pen came along.

Photo of ink stand and old ink pen

1. How would you feel about going through someone's room looking for clues? Would you worry about being caught?
2. Mary Beth and Mr. Grant worried how they would manage to work around Mr. Sadler. How did Mr. Grant do that? What do you think about his plan?
3. Peter prayed about every business he invested in. Why didn't he agree to invest in a factory that produced weapons?
4. Elsie stepped in the room while Mary Beth was paying bills and noticed Mary Beth seemed tense. Why do you think Mary Beth was stressed?
5. Read Luke 21:4 and I Timothy 6:17. Does God care how we use our money?
6. Aunt Louise and Mrs. Chandler disagreed on how to handle Ruth. Who do you agree with?
7. What indication did McDonald give Mary Beth that he didn't really care about her?

CHAPTER 14

1. What indication do we have that Peter is becoming fond of Mary Beth?
2. What do you think of how Peter handled the soldier who tried to start a fight?
3. What hint do you get that telegrams might not always work?
4. How do you think Peter and Mary Beth's courtship is going?
5. Why did Peter react when Mary Beth mentioned train accidents?
6. Look up the word discrepancy and write the definition.

CHAPTER 15

1. Explain why Peter was surprised to see Maud in his dining room.
2. Describe Maud.
3. How does Maud describe McDonald? Do you agree? Defend your answer.
4. Why didn't Maud know to inform her employer before she left?
5. What do you think of Mr. Roper's reaction to the news of counterfeit money?

CHAPTER 16

Ellen McCallie was tiny but energetic. She wore her dark hair in a tight bun and had incredible stamina. Ellen had a large family, yet she was active in the church, reaching out to anyone in need. Her home was open to anyone who came to Chattanooga whether pastor or peasant. Grace, her daughter, said she and her siblings were taught to be polite, even to annoying guests who came repeatedly. They were never allowed to ask when the visitor would leave because it might give the impression the person was unwelcome. During the war, Ellen took wounded soldiers into her home and nursed them back to health. Every day she prepared soup for her husband to take to the military hospital. She was a woman with a heart for God.

1. If you were Mary Beth, would you have tried to avoid Ellen McCallie? Why would she do that?
2. How do you feel about crying in public?
3. Why do you think Peter shared his own troubles?
4. Every banker fears a run on the bank. Describe what it is.
5. What do you think about Peter asking Maud to work for Mary Beth as a spy?

CHAPTER 17

1. Maud found another counterfeit bill. Compare Maud's reaction to the bill to Mary Beth's reaction.
2. How can you tell Bessie is tense?
3. Why did Peter question Bessie so closely?
4. How were Mary Beth and Peter different when they were alone at the bank?

CHAPTER 18

1. How do you think Mary Beth felt seeing McDonald after she expressed her deepest fear to Elsie? How would you have felt?
2. Note that Elsie didn't want McDonald to accompany Mary Beth alone. In that day, a young woman had escorts to protect her reputation. Being seen alone with a man could indicate she was courting him. In the light of the freedom we have today, we often scoff at such measures. However, being seen with someone of his reputation wouldn't be wise even today. How would you feel if your father protected you in that way? What rules do your parents have in place to protect you?
3. What indications did McDonald give that he liked the comforts of life?
4. Mary Beth unearthed pictures and mementos in her father's desk. How would that make you feel, knowing you would soon lose your father?
5. How important is that that the person who forged the money knew Peter ran the bank?

CHAPTER 19

Can you imagine your living room (sitting room) without a TV, radio, or computer? No one had iPads, mp3 players, or telephones, much less cell phones. People entertained themselves as they sat around the fire in the sitting room. At times, the ladies would play the piano or sing. Sometimes, a family member would read poetry while everyone listened. They also enjoyed parlor games and card games.

1. Who cared for Mary Beth's father while she attended the party?
2. Why did they have the party?
3. Contrast Peter and Mrs. Black.
4. What do you learn about Mrs. Chandler in this chapter?
5. What was Mr. Sadler doing when Mrs. Chandler came to the bank?
6. Why did Mr. Sadler back down?

CHAPTER 20

Houses had no electricity in the 1860s, which meant they used wind-up alarm clocks and clocks that ran on a pendulum with weights. Every night before going to bed, adults would wind their alarm clock and set it to ring. Winding once a day at the same time each day kept clocks running dependably.

1. Read the following verses and write about what life changes you can make to avoid anxiety. Phil 4:6–9
2. Why is death so jarring? Read Genesis 2:16
3. Have you ever lost a family member? How did you feel?
4. Mary Beth and Peter were both shocked by the sudden death of Sadler. Is grieving wrong? I Thess. 4:13.
5. Now that Sadler is dead, what problem do Mary Beth and Peter have?

Use these words: legal, retire, donning, charades, jittery, encounter, and escapade.

Name:_____

Chapter 20
Complete the crossword below

Across
2. nervous and shaky
4. a parlor game where you act out an event
6. in accordance with the law
7. meeting with someone

Down
1. go to bed,
3. an unusual event
5. the act of putting on

CHAPTER 21

1. Find the definition of betrayal in the dictionary.
2. How would you feel if someone you trusted betrayed you?
3. Read Psalm 55, especially verses 12 to 21. What happened to David?
4. Metaphor means comparing two items without the use of like or as. What metaphor does David use in verse 21 to describe his former friend?
5. Why did Peter need to interview bank employees?
6. What is foreshadowing? Give an example from this chapter.
7. What's behind Mary Beth's suspicion of Mrs. Phipps?

CHAPTER 22

1. Why would a cup of tea with sugar be refreshing?
2. Why do you think Mary Beth was no longer itching to get home to her father?
3. Describe Mrs. Sadler. How is she different than Mary Beth?
4. What do you think of them sedating Mrs. Sadler?
5. How does Mrs. Chandler react when she hears Sadler is dead?
6. What gift did Sadler give the Chandler family?

CHAPTER 23

Today in the United States, we have funeral homes that embalm the dead, and then offer large, plush rooms for viewing and chapels for the funeral. Funeral homes even escort the family to the burial site and complete the job after the family leaves. That's changing as more people choose cremation.

Historically, most people in the United States buried their dead within twenty-four hours after death so they wouldn't decay. Staying up with the body overnight was called the wake. The family wanted to prevent the body from being stolen by grave robbers, those who wanted to dissect the body, or those wanting to steal personal effects.

Burial actually comes from the Christian belief that the body will rise again, leaving an empty grave as a testimony.

Cremation was more common in Eastern cultures. A Hindu widow would usually throw herself on her husband's funeral fire, which is called sati. If she did not kill herself, the remaining family could refuse to support her.

During the Civil War, soldiers usually buried the fallen nearby the battlefield. Doctors had the ability to embalm, but it was time-consuming and expensive. Officers might be embalmed so the remains could be taken home for burial.

1. Why did Sadler's funeral appear so dreary?
2. Why couldn't Peter share the entire truth with the congregation at Sadler's funeral?
3. Why did Peter have the dream about his father?
4. What new rules might Peter put in place to protect the bank?
5. Why did Mary Beth suddenly agree to take Sadler's place?
6. What explanation did Dr. Smith give for Sadler's need for extra income?
7. Both Peter and Mary Beth wanted to know if Sadler's death could be murder. Explain the doctor's answer.

CHAPTER 24

1. What do you think about Sheriff Campbell?
2. What plan did Mary Beth have to determine how many counterfeit bills might be circulating?
3. What did Fanny have on her mind?
4. Which of the girls seemed the most reasonable?
5. Why didn't Anna keep her midnight visit from Sheriff Campbell?
6. How are Sargent Glass and Peter different?

CHAPTER 25

1. Compare Mary Beth and Peter's relationship in this chapter to the first part of the book.
2. Why did Peter agree to allow Mary Beth to interview Mrs. Fuller?
3. Why did Mrs. Fuller appear afraid when Mary Beth mentioned money?
4. Mary Beth had always been intimidated by Reverend McCallie's long face and deep-set eyes. Did her fear prove to be valid? Explain.
5. How did McCallie help Mary Beth?

CHAPTER 26

1. How did Anna's mood change when she got the anonymous letter? How would you have responded?
2. Mary Beth admitted to feeling guilt when she was away from her father enjoying herself. Explain why she feels that way.
3. Mary Beth took charge of the situation when she and Mrs. Chandler found the mess in the library. Why didn't Mrs. Chandler take a more active role?
4. Why did Peter think of Ruth when he saw the office disaster?
5. How did Mary Beth know Ruth was holding back?

CHAPTER 27

1. What do you think of Peter and Mary Beth's plan to search for counterfeit money?
2. What did Mary Beth do when she found a forged bill? Was that a good solution?
3. In the 1800s, wealthy women often carried calling cards that bore their name. (The cards resembled business cards people often carry today.) If the friend wasn't home, ladies would leave the card with the maid or butler. When the printer asked Mary Beth if she was ready to print her calling cards, how did she answer?
4. Mary Beth finally speaks to Dr. Bell about Glass, which shows growth in her personality. She would have never done that when the story began. What do you think about Bell's reaction?
5. How could the state of Tennessee solve Peter's problem?

CHAPTER 28

Mr. Roper's health continues to decline, and he becomes less able to communicate. Notice he still wants to help and insists Peter report bank news. He demonstrates a person who is other-centered, following Jesus's example. Jesus left all his glory and came to earth to die for our sins. He didn't come to be served, but to serve and to give his life as a ransom for many. Think about how you can put others first like he did.

Doctors in the 1800s thought of death as vital powers waning, so they often gave stimulants like caffeine to dying people. Also, they were hesitant to sedate since pain appeared to stimulate vital powers. Dr. Smith chose to give Mr. Roper stimulants when he appeared to be going into a coma. This technique can work temporarily until the heart fails completely.

1. Notice Mr. Roper's comment that Sadler was secretive. Read John 3:19–20 and explain why.
2. How can the information you learned about secretive people impact your life?
3. How did Mary Beth respond to the medical emergency with her father? Why?
4. Mary Beth worried about the bank. How does Peter answer? Do you agree with his decision to stay with Mary Beth?
5. A vigil like this can be very difficult for the family. How did Peter and Mary Beth cope? What does their relationship look like?
6. How does sleep impact your health? (Research the answer.)
7. Compare Mary Beth's reaction to the bombing with the minister's

CHAPTER 29

1. Has Mary Beth's faith improved? Explain your answer.
2. Hearing is the last sense to leave the body. So, caregivers should be careful what they say even when the patient is unresponsive. What does Mary Beth say to her father?
3. Have you ever noticed people whisper when they talk about death? The conversation Peter and Mary Beth have at Roper's bedside is intense. What would you be feeling if you were Mary Beth?
4. Peter joined Mary Beth as her father is slipping away. What did Peter say when Mary Beth mentions the bank? Do you agree? Why or why not?
5. Mary Beth felt alone and believed no one cared after the funeral. Was she accurate? How might her thoughts reflect grieving? See Psalm 88
6. How did Peter's priorities change at the end of the chapter?

CHAPTER 30

1. Why couldn't Mary Beth sleep at the Chandler home?
2. Describe the young man Mary Beth saw.
3. Why do you think Ruth left a message in the woods?
4. Mary Beth wasn't happy Peter sent Maud to spy on Mary Beth. How would you feel if someone spied on you?
5. Why does Ruth speak more easily with Mary Beth?
6. Can you guess who the midnight visitor is?

CHAPTER 31

Chattanooga didn't have a hospital until after Nashville fell to the Union. The railroad brought mobs of wounded soldiers as well as refugees from the battle. Citizens took over an abandoned warehouse that sat beside the Tennessee River and turned it into Newsome Hospital. Emily Todd Helm, half-sister to Mary Lincoln, stayed in Chattanooga at the time. She helped city officials and Chattanooga women make mattresses from straw and fabric. The military took over the hospital and assigned a doctor to run it. Dr. Milo Smith worked there also.

Nurses who volunteered at Newsome Hospital had to cook meals for the patients as well as clean and care for them. They cooked a full diet, half diet, and liquids only for those very ill.

1. How did Mary Beth find comfort the next morning?
2. Contrast how Mary Beth felt about her mother with how Ruth felt about hers.
3. Why was Peter dismayed by Mary Beth's announcement?
4. How do you think Mary Beth will investigate at the hospital?

CHAPTER 32

1. Do you think Peter will obey Sheriff Campbell and stop snooping? Why?
2. Why did Mary Beth react so strongly to her first patient's death?
3. Why do you think Mary Beth was drawn to Major General Connelly?
4. Do you think Peter's concerns for Mary Beth's safety are realistic? Why or why not?

CHAPTER 33

1. What did Mary Beth learn as she perused the unused portion of Newsome Hospital?
2. What regrets did Connelly have?
3. Why did McDonald turn nasty and shoot at Peter?
4. What puzzle did Peter solve in his library?

CHAPTER 34

1. Why didn't Peter report McDonald earlier?
2. Why was Mary Beth reluctant to share with Connelly?
3. What did Mary Beth learn from Connelly? How did that change her perspective?
4. How can this same truth impact your life?

CHAPTER 35

1. How did Peter and Mary Beth feel when they found the counterfeit money?
2. Why did George Bell kill Mr. Allen?
3. How did they find out George Bell was the counterfeiter?
4. How did Connelly know Mary Beth needed help?

CHAPTER 36

Dr. Smith probably listened to Mrs. Chandler's heart when he examined her. The stethoscope was invented by Rene Laennec in 1816. He didn't want to put his ear on a lady's chest to hear her heartbeat. He rolled up a piece of paper and placed on her chest, putting his ear on the other end. Doing that allowed him to listen without touching. Later, he made a wooden tube rather than using paper each time.

ACTIVITY

Roll up a piece of paper into a tube and listen to another person's heart. Get a stopwatch and count the beats for one minute. The normal heart rate is 50 to 100 beats per minute for an adult. A child can be anywhere from 80 to 130.

1. Why did Mrs. Chandler have stomach problems? Do you think she regretted her secretive actions that brought the sheriff to visit?
2. Tell what happened after she took her burdens to God.
3. Why would Peter hide his pain from Mary Beth? Is this the same as Mrs. Chandler hiding her actions regarding Sadler? Why or why not?
4. Who was George Bell and why was he important?

5. Who was Ruth's new friend? How did that friendship explain her hesitancy to go to Savannah?
6. Who took Peter's signature off the letter?
7. How did the cotton convince Mary Beth to look further for the culprit?

APPENDIX 1: MANAGING YOUR MONEY

INTRODUCTION

Mary Beth and Peter kept a budget to ensure they did not spend more money than they earned. A budget is a spending plan listing expenses and income. We should spend less than we earn and save extra income for vacations or unexpected bills.

Spending too much creates a problem. Peter would have to sell his possessions to pay his bills or go into debt. When a person borrows money and goes into debt, the money must be repaid with interest. In other words, the lender charges money on what is borrowed.

Prov. 22:7 "The rich rules over the poor, and the borrower becomes the lender's slave."

Notice the word "slave" above. Choosing to go into debt puts the borrower at the mercy of the lender. Good financial managers save money and pay cash rather than enslave themselves. The exception to the rule is buying a house, because a house increases in value and is usually worth more than the original price. However, a wise person will make extra payments on the principal, or the cost of the house, which reduces the overall interest and pays the loan off early.

LESSON 1

Money received as salary has to go a lot of places. Some expenses are monthly, and some are not. For instance, usually people pay for their car insurance twice a year. A simple system uses pretend envelopes. The envelope for transportation would need to earn a little every month to cover the twice-yearly insurance bill. On the other hand, groceries are usually bought every week, so that money will be spent right away.

The beauty of this envelope budget is money can be moved around. Food or clothes money left at the end of the month can be moved to another account or saved for something bigger. The only accounts not to rob are the ones with a big bill coming, like car insurance.

Here is a list of expenses and recommended percentages. Remember percentages are based on 100%. 10% is 10/100 or .10. 40% is 40/100 or .40.

Suppose the income is $2500 a month. Five percent can be spent on clothes. Multiply 2500 by .05 to find how much to put in the clothing envelope.

$2500. x .05 = $125.

Using this formula, figure out how much can be spent in each category with a $3000 a month income.

Housing/utilities—30%

Housing includes money for homeowners' or rental insurance, home repairs, and utilities (water bill, electric bill, trash. These costs may be included in rental fees.)

Clothing—5%

Toiletries can be included here, although some people put this in the grocery account.

Car—10%

This will include car insurance, gas for the car, and car repairs.

Groceries—15%

Cleaning supplies and paper items will be added here.

Misc.—15%

Doctor bills, stamps for mailing, or other irregular expenses are in this category.

Savings—15% or more

Put money here for vacations, large purchases, or emergencies.

Tithe—10 % or more as you choose

LESSON 2: DISTRIBUTING YOUR INCOME ACROSS THE ENVELOPES

Your income is $2500 per month. Divide the money into pretend envelopes by using a spreadsheet like the one on the next page. (There are also programs to keep track of money, but they work along the same principles.) Fill in how much to put in each category each payday. Put the total at the bottom to make sure the allocations equal the amount earned. (This amount may change during the year based on several factors.) After income is distributed, write the amount on a special page for each category. Clothing is done.

Category	Jan	Feb	Mar	Apr	May	Jun	Jul	Aug	Sep	Oct	Nov	Dec
Housing												
Clothes	125											
Car												
Groc.												
Misc												
Savings												
Tithe												
Total	3000											

LESSON 3

In this lesson, use the amounts from the last lesson and plug them into the correct envelopes. Then keep track of how much money is in each. The total amount should be the amount in the checking account. The trick is not to spend money if the envelope is empty. Or to borrow from monthly envelopes. This spreadsheet is similar to a checkbook register.

This first envelope will be **Housing**:

Date	Income	Description	Spent	Total
Jan				

The second, **Clothing**:

Date	Income	Description	Spent	Total
Jan				

Car:

Date	Income	Description	Spent	Total
Jan				

Groceries:

Date	Income	Description	Spent	Total
Jan				

Misc:

Date	Income	Description	Spent	Total
Jan				

Savings:

Date	Income	Description	Spent	Total
Jan				

Tithe:

Date	Income	Description	Spent	Total
Jan				

LESSON 4

Now, let's work with the individual envelopes. Money has been deposited in the grocery envelope. List the transactions.

1. $25.76 spent for groceries on Jan. 5
2. Buy milk for $3.29 on Jan. 8
3. Get contact lens solution on Jan. 12 for $5.99.

Add up the amount after each transaction.

Date	Income	Description	Spent	Total
1-Jan	375			375
5-Jan		Groceries	25.76	

Let's pretend at the end of March there is a negative balance in the misc. account because of a doctor bill and medication which took more than planned. Remember, as long as there is money in the other envelopes, you will be okay. Just move money around.

1. Clothing has $15, which can be moved.
2. Groceries has an extra $25 to move.
3. Find the total.

Now note what has been moved from one envelope to another.

Misc.

Date	Income	Description	Spent	Total
March				-40
31-March	15	From clothing		
31-March	25	From groceries		

Clothing

Date	Income	Description	Spent	Total
March				
31-March		To Misc	15	0

Groceries

Date	Income	Description	Spent	Total
March				
31-March		To Misc	25	0

LESSON 5

1. Price nearby apartments. How much income is needed to afford to live there?
2. Pick out a car and find out the price for it used and new. If a loan on the car has 5% interest, how much is the full cost for the car? (Also ask about the price of insurance for the car per month.)
3. During the Civil War, a plumber in the city would make $1.88 per hour. How much would that be per month if working forty hours per week?
4. Once the salary is figured, take 30% for housing. How much could they spend on rent?
5. How much could they spend on clothes?
6. They need clothes for their job. How much would they have left if they bought a tie for 50 cents, a shirt for $1.50, pants for $2.00, and shoes for $1.00?

LESSON 6: DEBT PART 1

Americans tend to buy appliances or furniture right away rather than saving money and buying the items with cash. Credit cards make that possible because the card company lends money to the credit card user. However, they charge anywhere from 18% interest to 24% interest on purchases if you don't pay in full the first month. Plus, they add large fees if you are late on your payments. Because the interest adds up, it's hard to pay off what you have purchased because the bill grows.

1. Using a credit card, you purchased $1000 of furniture for your apartment, which you intended to pay off. However, even though you make monthly payments, your balance stays the same because you paid for lunches and other expenses with your new credit card. Over the course of a year, you paid late twice, and the company added $35 each time to your bill. Plus, they added 24% interest to the original $1000. How much do you owe at the end of the year?

2. Use the answer to #1 for the second year. You only pay late once, but the credit card company adds another 24% interest to your bill. How much do you owe at the end of the second year?

Strive to stay out of debt. One idea is to make a car payment to the envelope after a car is paid off. When a new car is needed, the money has been saved. A new car is not a good investment because it drops in price the moment you leave the car lot and becomes a used car. It's best to buy a good used car with fifteen thousand or so miles because you are paying for the value you get.

3. If you saved $235 each month, how long would you have to save to buy a used car? A new car?

4. Pick out a new car to purchase. If you finance that over 10 years at 5% interest, how much would you pay in all?

A house increases in value faster than the interest on your loan (unless interest rates are very high). However, an extra principal payment with each house payment will pay the house off early.

One way to get out of debt is to pay off the smallest debt, and then to use all the extra money to pay down the next smallest. Continue until you are debt free.

Lesson 7: Debt Part II

Your mother gave you a credit card for you to buy lunch five days a week when school started in August, and she allowed you seven dollars a day. You have to make the monthly payments, which is 4% of the balance. The card company charges you 24% interest a year.

Look at the chart on the next page. The first column tells the month, the second gives the purchases for the month. The third shows the interest added and the fourth shows the payment you must make when the bill comes. The last column tells how much of your bill remains.

1. Go to row #1 (use a ruler or a slip of paper under the row to keep your place). The first month you bought $151.76 in lunches, and the second column shows the credit card added $1.52 in interest. The first month the amount unpaid is $153.18

2. Drop down to December or month 5. The first row shows you spent the same amount. How much was your monthly payment? How much do you owe altogether?

3. Go to May or month 10. How much interest do you add that month? What is your monthly payment? How much do you owe altogether?

4. Drop down to month 24, which means you've had the card for two years only adding lunch. How much interest do you have to pay? What is your monthly payment? How much do you owe altogether?

5. Go to month 35. At this point, you've had the credit card for almost three years. How much interest do you pay that month? What is your monthly payment? How much do you owe altogether? How does that amount compare to the amount you spend each month?

6. Why did your debt grow? What could you do instead of use a credit card?

Dig Your Credit Card Hole

First Purchase	$	-
Interest Rate	24%	per Year
Minimum Monthly Pmt	4.00%	per Month
Spending	$ 151.67	per Month
		$7 per weekday for lunch

Month	Purchases	Interest	Monthly Payment	Unpaid
Beginning	-			-
1	151.67	1.52	-	153.18
2	151.67	4.58	6.13	303.30
3	151.67	7.58	12.13	450.42
4	151.67	10.53	18.02	594.60
5	151.67	13.41	23.78	735.89
6	151.67	16.23	29.44	874.35
7	151.67	19.00	34.97	1,010.05
8	151.67	21.72	40.40	1,143.03
9	151.67	24.38	45.72	1,273.35
10	151.67	26.98	50.93	1,401.07
11	151.67	29.54	56.04	1,526.23
12	151.67	32.04	61.05	1,648.89
13	151.67	34.49	65.96	1,769.10
14	151.67	36.90	70.76	1,886.90
15	151.67	39.25	75.48	2,002.34
16	151.67	41.56	80.09	2,115.48
17	151.67	43.83	84.62	2,226.35
18	151.67	46.04	89.05	2,335.01
19	151.67	48.22	93.40	2,441.49
20	151.67	50.35	97.66	2,545.85
21	151.67	52.43	101.83	2,648.11
22	151.67	54.48	105.92	2,748.33
23	151.67	56.48	109.93	2,846.55
24	151.67	58.45	113.86	2,942.80
25	151.67	60.37	117.71	3,037.13
26	151.67	62.26	121.49	3,129.57
27	151.67	64.11	125.18	3,220.16
28	151.67	65.92	128.81	3,308.94
29	151.67	67.70	132.36	3,395.95
30	151.67	69.44	135.84	3,481.21
31	151.67	71.14	139.25	3,564.77
32	151.67	72.81	142.59	3,646.66
33	151.67	74.45	145.87	3,726.91
34	151.67	76.05	149.08	3,805.55
35	151.67	77.63	152.22	3,882.63
36	151.67	79.17	155.31	3,958.16
37	151.67	80.68	158.33	4,032.18
38	151.67	82.16	161.29	4,104.72
39	151.67	83.61	164.19	4,175.81

APPENDIX 2—HISTORY OF MONEY

EARLY FORMS OF MONEY

The history of money reveals how people lived and worked together in society. In Genesis, Eve gave birth to two boys, Cain and Able. Cain grew up and found his niche in farming. Able cared for flocks. Just imagine what happened (this is not recorded in the Bible) when Cain needed milk, which would come from Able's cow. They probably met and decided how many vegetables or wheat to exchange for a certain amount of milk. The same thing probably happened when Cain wanted steak. He and his brother would negotiate how much to exchange. Let's say Eve baked great bread, and she would agree to exchange several loaves of bread for Cain's produce. This is called **bartering**. Bartering means to trade by exchanging goods rather than money. Sometimes people still barter. For example, a hairdresser can style a friend's hair in exchange for getting tax returns filed.

Problems emerged with bartering. For instance, imagine a seamstress who needed fresh bread, who offered to sew for the baker in exchange for bread. The baker refused because he didn't need her services. That means the seamstress had to find someone else to barter with or to go without the bread she needed. A small community might not have two bakers, so the seamstress needed another way to get her bread.

When bartering didn't work out, people used other items instead. Any article offered for exchange had to be something society valued—an item that could be used for different jobs. For instance, women enjoyed decorating themselves, so they would like anything they could string into necklaces: pretty rocks, gemstones, shells, or gold nuggets.

Here's a list of objects people used for bartering: salt, tea, gold, silver, cows, dried grain, arrowhead, hair pin, fish hook, animal skins/fur, perfumes, musket balls, spices, and weapons. During the Roman times, people liked how salt made their food taste, so the government paid their soldiers in salt. That's where we get the phrase, "not worth its salt."

Gold had many uses, so people valued it more than other things. However, if gold dust was offered in exchange, the other person would have to look closely. Some gold dust contained more gold than others.

1. What is bartering?
2. Name some objects used in exchange?
3. What do you have that you could use to barter?

COINS

Eventually, governments made coins from metals. Gold was the most popular, but some coins had copper, silver, or nickel. The value was in the coin itself, because people wanted gold. The government would set the standard of purity and choose how much gold went into each coin.

Have you ever seen an old movie where a person offered a coin in payment, and the potential seller would bite down on it? The coin was being checked to be sure it was gold. Gold is soft, and if the coin is actually gold, the person's teeth would leave an impression.

Making coins: Gold is heated until it's liquid and then pressed into a mold. The mold usually has an image of the governor or king. Remember when a man asked Jesus if he should pay taxes. In answer, Jesus took a coin, held it up, and asked who was depicted on the coin. Of course, the man answered the emperor. In Matthew 22:21, Jesus instructed, "Therefore render to Caesar the things that are Caesar's, and to God the things that are God's."

Romans 12:2 says, "Do not be **conformed** to this world, but be transformed by the renewal of your mind, that by testing you may discern what is the will of God, what is good and acceptable and perfect."

The word conformed means to press into a mold, the way they stamped gold coins. God doesn't want us to look like the world.

1. Name some metals that governments use for coins.
2. Describe how coins are made.
3. What does conform mean?

BANKS

Imagine starting a tailoring business, which makes or alters clothes for people. However, in order to start, tools need to be bought. Today, we have sewing machines, but in the past people sewed by hand. They would still need needles, fabric, thread, and measuring tape.

94

How can someone get money to begin tailoring? People would borrow from a wealthy person and then repay the *loan* as the business grew. What if there is no one to borrow from? That's where banks came in. Banks would loan the money, and the business would repay the loan over a set number of years. However, the banks charged a fee for using the money, and it's called *interest*. Interest rates vary, but banks usually have a *prime rate* they offer to their best customers.

If a bank gives a $100 loan with 4% interest, the 4% paid to the bank would fund their business and pay their employees. Imagine a bank offering loans for many upcoming businesses. A bank would therefore be helping the community grow to provide goods and services for its citizens.

In Europe, the Medici family set up a chain of banks, and money could be moved from bank to bank. The Bank of England worked the same way. That did not happen in the US until later, because Andrew Jackson didn't not want a national bank. In the 1800s, banks tended to have individual charters from the state or city.

1. What is interest?
2. Define loan.
3. What is prime rate?

PAPER MONEY

Do you remember when you were younger how special you felt when someone handed you a five-dollar bill? However, the paper has no intrinsic value and can be easily forged. Governments tended to issue paper money during times of stress, like war, when prices went up. Later, when prices stabilized, they would return to coins.

However, during the Civil War, the United States made the permanent transition from coins to paper money. War causes prices to go up, which is called *inflation*, because the government must make bullets, feed, and clothe soldiers, and pay the men who fight. In 1862, the North passed a legal tender law that said the dollar was worth a dollar's worth of gold but could not be exchanged for coins during the war. The Union also chose the size and color of the bills. Green represented prosperity and was harder for forgers to copy, so they chose green. The mints added other colors in 2003.

The Confederacy had another set of problems. They had all the problems war causes without the resources the North had. As the South was largely agricultural, the people didn't have the industry and transportation their opponent had. Raising money in gold, or *specie*, presented a problem. They seized the gold from mints in Louisiana, North Carolina, and Georgia. Several states gave large sums of money, and individuals offered grain or fabric for the soldiers. Many women cut their hair and sold it to Europe for wigs, so they could contribute the funds to the Confederacy. However, donations didn't cover all their expenses, so officials chose to sell bonds. Wealthy citizens and large banks lent their gold to the government, and the government promised to pay the loans back with interest. After the war, the government would owe the banks a lot, which was good for banks. Banks needed currency for spending, so they began printing their own money in various sizes shapes and colors. States and cities released money too, and all that paper created a confusing mess for citizens. The confederacy printed bills that bore interest to pay their debts. However, they never passed a legal tender law. If they needed money, they printed more, hoping to win the war, so they could retire the debt. When the Confederacy lost the war, all the banks that loaned them money failed. Plus, all the Confederate money was useless, and many people burned it in the streets.

1. What is inflation?
2. Define specie.

INTERESTING FACTS ABOUT MONEY

- Both the Union and Confederacy endured counterfeiting during the Civil War.
- In colonial times, wealthy people coined their own money.
- After the revolutionary war, the United States produced coin to exchange, but no paper money. State-chartered banks would produce banknotes to use for exchange, but they were confusing. If the bank failed, which often happened, the bills were worthless.
- Wildcat banks had no specie, but merely issued bank notes worth nothing.

SALARIES IN THE CIVIL WAR

1860

Bricklayer—$1.53 day
Painter—$1.97 day
Fireman—$1.33 day
Plumber ——$1.88 day

Prices in the Civil War

Boy's hat—$.25
Skirt—$1.75
Umbrella—$.50
Collar—$.15
Collar and cuffs—$.25
Ladies gloves—$.50

- Fiat money has no precious metals to authenticate its worth but is valuable because of a government decree that it can be used to pay debts.
- Today paper money is 75% cotton 25% linen rather than paper. Security threads and watermarks run through larger bills to protect against counterfeiting.
- It costs 42 cents to make a dollar bill for circulation.
- Money printed in the US can always be used regardless of its age. However, in other countries money expires, and the bearer must exchange the bill at the bank.
- After Lincoln died, his family found a five-dollar Confederate note in his billfold.
- The government hires artists to design the pictures and designs on both coins and bills.

APPENDIX 3: TEACHER'S MANUAL/ANSWER KEY

TEACHING A SENSE OF TIME

An eight-year-old boy once spread his arms and said, "I've never seen anything like that in my whole life."

Life abounds with interesting things and that child has only begun to glimpse God's creation. Children often ask adults, "Back when you were a kid, did people …"

The past is a black hole for kids. All of that happened before they were born, and they assume you have been here forever. Kids may ask adults questions like "What did Abraham look like?"

Children need a grid to hang a few facts on, and a time line works for that. They don't always need the details, but rather a date or two to create structure. Add a little color and a personality to make it stick. Here's an example:

Begin with a turning point in history, such as October 31, 1517, the beginning of the Reformation.

The start of World War II is another turning point date.

Draw a few pictures or make a wall chart. Add events here and there on the time line as history is learned. Any event taught can be placed before or after those big ones marked out. Special events in children's lives can be added as well. Plus, timelines also teach math and sequencing.

TEACHING KIDS TO THINK

"Come let us reason together. Though your sins are scarlet, they shall be white as snow." Isaiah 1:18

Note that God asks us to *reason* with him.

"In the beginning was the word, and the word with God and was God." John 1:1

"Word" here is logos, from which we get the word logic.

The Bible clearly shows God, Jahveh (Jehovah, the name God asked his people to call him), is reason, logic. Francis Bacon believed God created a reasonable universe, therefore we can ask questions and discover God's work. That means using the world as God intended in Genesis to allow man to rule and have dominion over nature.

As a result of that belief, Bacon created the scientific method that we have used to modernize our world. We can look around at what we see—airplanes, cars, microwaves, the internet—to see how the scientific method assisted us in building what we use every day.

However, the modern world view has moved far from belief in God. That's a problem because ideas matter. Typically, school-age children only accumulate facts. However, because we live in the post-Christian era, messages we all hear in the media no longer reflect a Biblical worldview. Children should be able to sort through ideas presented to them, so critical thinking has been included in this guide.

A young child can start reasoning by answering compare and contrast questions. Some children have problems with similarities while others have problems with differences. Give them time to think and be willing to walk them through the issue with questions. Lead a child through the hard stuff with a snippet of encouragement. Think of it as a trail of breadcrumbs. It also helps to cover categories like living, nonliving, transportation, communication, building materials, and so on. Those categories give a child a grid to use for organization, so they can sort and file.

EXERCISES:

How are a tree and a rock different? This should be pretty easy, but some children will still need to walk through this an inch at a time. Keep asking questions. **Which one is alive? Which one grows? Which one has parts?** (leaves, branches, stems) You may find a rock with two different types of material like sedimentary rock with volcanic. If you do, point that out. **Which one is harder? Which one produces food?**

How are they the same? Ask them where you might find a rock and tree. Usually outside, but sometimes you'll have rocks in a museum and trees in a solarium. Allow them to brainstorm, even if it's wrong. Make it fun by having a contest or thinking of silly stuff.

How is bread like a mailbox? There may not be too many similarities here. But brainstorm. Both are nonliving. **Are they the same color? Hardness? Uses? Places you find them?**

How are they different? This may be easier after doing the first one. One is outside and the other inside. One is hard, the other is soft. One is for communication, the other is food.

How is a bush like a tree? Ask about location, parts, color, uses, food, growth, flowering.

How are they different? This is harder because they are similar. Compare sizes and uses in the landscape.

How is ice cream like steak? Both of them are food. They provide energy for your body. You would find them in the kitchen and buy them at the store.

How are they different? One is eaten hot and the other cold. Steak is eaten with a fork and knife, and a spoon is used eat ice cream. Ice cream has sugar, steak is mostly protein and fat.

How is a cat like a person? Both are warm-blooded, both eat meat, both bear live young, both communicate, both bathe themselves.

How are they different? A cat lives by instinct, and a person is made in God's image. People don't scratch the carpet like cats. People bathe in water and wear clothes. People have a sense of eternity and a desire for God.

Have classroom discussions. Ask children their opinion and then ask why? You might learn something about how they think and be able to see misconceptions. Remember children see the world as it relates to them. If they grew up in an apartment with a dog, they may assume everyone lives in an apartment and have a dog.

Discourage yes and no arguments. Have them express why with facts and reasons, which is tough. They will learn to express their thoughts in words and also reveal who they are and how they think. Ask "Why do you think you should sit in the front seat of the car?" "Why do you want meatloaf instead of hot dogs?" "Why do you want to wear that?"

Ask questions for them to discuss. Here's an example. A girl in her preteens was shopping with her mother at a grocery store. She saw another lady with a baby in the aisle with baking items. The baby sat in the lady's cart and reached out for a package of sugar, pulling on the paper where it was sealed. The girl envisioned the baby pulling hard enough for the sugar package to tear open and spill. Should the girl make the baby stop? Tell the baby's mother? Or do nothing? Why? Make them defend their answer.

Here's another example. A man was looking for a gift to give his wife. He was in a crowded aisle of a party store, and a child ran past him. The man backed up to get out of the child's way, and he brushed a vase on a shelf behind him. The vase fell to the floor and broke. What should the man do?

MOVIES AND TV

Our culture is now post-Christian, and we must teach children to examine all the media that bombards us. Artists attempt to influence society, and many of them want to promote a humanistic world view. Even a cartoon can have a message we don't want to communicate. Satan can use any media to plant lies in a child's mind. Take, for instance, the movie *Frozen*. The main character has the ability to freeze things, and her parents see that ability as a problem. In essence, they don't accept how she is made. Of course, parents should accept children's abilities and temperaments, but homosexuals use this same argument too. They will say the Creator made them long for the same sex, and therefore, they have no choice. If we look at Genesis, we see God made us male and female to multiply, producing the next generation. So, homosexuality falls outside of God's design, and the Bible labels that lifestyle inappropriate. All of us have our own tendencies to sin, but the Bible calls us to rise above our bodily urges.

Help the children to see the meaning behind the movie *Frozen* and compare that with Scripture. God does make people different. In fact, Romans 12 talks about spiritual gifts. The entire body of Christ needs each gift, and we should allow people to use their gifts. This movie gives you a chance to talk about acceptance in the context of truth.

1. Here are some questions to help children evaluate media. What is the overall tone? Playful, educational, mysterious, nostalgic, educational, hopeful, sensual, analytical? What elements cause you to make this choice?

2. How are Christians portrayed? With respect? Disdain? Ridicule? Superstitious? Give reasons for your answer.

3. What other religions are represented? Witches? Compare how they portrayed to Christians.

4. What issues arise? (social, political, religion, truth, welfare, worship, freedom) What reasons are given for the positions characters take on the issues? What position does Scripture take on that issue?

5. How did they portray the relationships of male and female? Lifelong marriage as described in Mark 10: 6–10? Did you see flirtation? Inappropriate conversation?

6. Which is emphasized feelings or facts? Compare how God wants us to view feelings and facts. (See 1 Cor. 5:1–9 with 2 Cor. 2: 1-11. Rom.12: 15–16)

7. How do they portray mothers? Parents? Compare how God sees women in Pro. 31 to how they portray women.

8. What overall message comes through? Compare that to the Bible

9. If they portray religion, how does religion impact the life of the characters? How does Christianity impact our lives? See Romans 12:1–2

10. What value is placed on life? Unborn babies? Disabled? Elderly? Poor?

11. Are people portrayed as bad, good, or neutral? Give examples. Compare to how the Bible describes people.

12. Describe the view of justice and compare to God's view. (proportional justice, as seen in Exodus 21: 23–25) Did they portray mercy? How?

13. How do they portray businessmen vs. poor people? See 2 Thess. l 3: 10–12.

14. How do they deal with money and wealth? I Tim. 6:10 and Matt. 6:33

15. How are personal possessions viewed? Compare to Exodus 20:15.

16. Describe those in authority and compare to God's standard for leaders in Matthew 20: 8.

17. Do they make unwarranted assumptions? Don't be afraid to ask about assumptions even if the topic is science or history. Name them and tell why they are unwarranted.

18. Do you get an idea of the writer's ideal society? How does that compare with Romans 13?

19. Do they describe a cause/effect world or does inappropriate behavior get rewarded? See Galatians 6:7–9.

20. Do they intend to persuade? If so, did you feel swayed? What elements impacted you the most? Compare their position to the Bible. See Acts 17:11.

BIBLE STORIES

Analyze the stories. For example, let's take the Bible story about the woman with the issue of blood. (Probably endometriosis. Note that any bleeding would make her unclean.) She had been to many doctors and suffered for years because they couldn't cure her. When Jesus came to town, she joined the crowd to see him, but didn't call attention to herself. Instead she reached out and touched the tassels (hem of the garment means the tassels, which have knots to represent Old Testament laws) on his garment. When she touches his clothing, she is healed. But Jesus knew she touched him, and he called her to come forward. When she did, he told her that her faith healed her.

Sample questions:
Where was her husband?
How did she know Jesus could heal?
Why didn't she want to come forward and ask Jesus to heal her?
How would you feel coming to Jesus in front of a crowd?

Why did Jesus insist on talking to her?

Did touching Jesus heal her?

What is faith?

An older child and Socratic questions.

Socrates developed these hundreds of years ago. He was a Greek philosopher, and you can find more about him online.

1. Clarification—What do you mean?

   *Make sure you understand the question. Be aware of the child's developmental stage in life and think about how that relates to the question being asked.

2. Assumptions—What assumption are you making?

   *If you ask a man if he stopped beating his wife, the assumption is that he is beating his wife.

3. Reason/Evidence—How do you prove that?

   *If someone claimed a tomato is poison (people used to believe that), you ask for evidence. What compound is in the tomato is dangerous? What does that compound do to the body? Show how the scientific proof uses the scientific method.

4. Perspectives—Who benefits?

   *If the Senate passes a law exempting themselves from taxes, clearly only the Senate benefits.

5. Implication/Consequences—What is the outcome of _____?

   *If the Senate passes a law exempting themselves from taxes, will that mean the rest of the public has to pay more? What other things might happen?

   What might happen if Congress singled out a category of people and entitled them to money? More people would find a way to fit in the category because they wanted the money, creating dependence on the government. This outcome wouldn't be what the person who penned the law intended.

   About the question—What makes you ask that? How does that apply to _____?

   This is similar to #1, but it further clarifies. Sometimes a child will ask a question that seems off topic. This will help show how the student makes the connection.

LITERATURE

Have the children compare and contrast characters. A character's actions often reveal personality. So have the children interpret the signals the writer gives. Was the person shy? Outgoing? Determined? Stubborn? Fearful? How does that compare with another character in the story? Did the character show respect for Christianity? Did that person obey the Bible? What did they believe and how does that compare to Scripture? This can be done with characters in this book.

CHARACTER STUDY

Identify the personalities: Four Types of Temperaments

a. *Melancholy—Shy (Organizer, see Gilden and Goldfarb)*
   i. Strengths: plan everything with care, thoughtful, considerate, schedule oriented, highly detailed, and creative, can work independently, cautious, inventive

   ii. Faults: moody, get stuck on one thing and can't move on, easily depressed, put things off, hard to please, can be a martyr.

   iii. Shyness body language: eyes on the floor, quiet, no eye contact, limbs held tightly to the body, avoiding physical contact, rejuvenates alone.

b. *Sanguine—Outgoing (Socializer)*
   i. Strengths: warm and fun loving, makes friends easily, confident, gracious, spontaneous, life of the party.

   ii. Weaknesses: loud, impulsive, lack of follow through if things get boring, shameless, competitive, often late, exaggerate, impulsive talker, easily distracted.

   iii. Body language of an outgoing person: smiling, loves people, life of the party, talking to strangers, hands and arms in open posture, chattering. Gathers energy from people.

c. *Phlegmatic—Tend toward shyness (Stabilizer)*
   i. Strengths: relaxed, peaceful, consistent, affectionate, diplomatic, rational curious, observant

   ii. Weaknesses: lazy, lacks discipline, stubborn, passive-aggressive, not goal-oriented, shy, fear change, compromise too easily, nonparticipant, sarcastic, discouraging

   iii. Body language: quiet exterior without the appearance of tension

d. *Choleric—Outgoing (Mobilizer)*
   i. Strengths: job oriented, wants to get things done, practical, logical, knows how to accomplish the job, knows how inspire people, cool under pressure

   ii. Weaknesses: loud, can be critical even a bully, logical, discuss facts, insensitive because they want to get the job done, has great ideas that work, not compassionate.

   iii. Body language: much like outgoing. Firm set to the jaw, frowning if someone disagrees.

Have the class identify the temperament of each character.

1. What characteristics show that person was a choleric, and so on?
   a. Which temperament are you?

   b. Have you ever met a melancholy? Describe the person.

    c. Discuss how a melancholy and a choleric might clash.

    d. How would a phlegmatic clash with a sanguine?

2. Identify the mood. Have the child identify which emotion the character demonstrated.
   You may have to give clues to get them started

    a. Was the person angry? How could you tell?
   reddened face, scowl, yelling.

    b. Did anyone exhibit sadness?
   hunched over, tears, frown, droopy features.

    c. Did any of your characters flirt? What body language let you know that?

    d. How would a fearful person act?
   possibly trembling, unwilling to leave, tearful, expressed concern over safety

    e. Did any of your characters display shock after receiving bad news? How did they act?
   unable to process the news, deep breathing, gasp.

    f. Did anyone in the story attempt to get revenge? What clues did you have?

    g. Was anyone in the story in a hurry? How could you tell?

    h. How would a happy person act?
   open arms, may not keep feet on the floor, smiling

    i. Was anyone sleepy? What behavior let you know? Why might they be sleepy?

    j. Did any of the characters hate their circumstances and want to get away? What did they do? How did they treat others in that situation?

    k. Did one of the characters fall in love? How did they act?

    l. Did any of your characters seem lazy? What did they do to let you know?

    m. Was anyone stubborn? How did you know?

    n. Did any of the characters show moral weakness? What actions did they display?

3. Relationship cues

    a. Share an argument in the story. How could you tell the characters were angry? What wording let you know this wasn't friendly?

    b. Did anyone have a tense conversation that wasn't a full-blown argument? How did you know?

    c. What does a friendly conversation look like?

    d. Did anyone give orders without listening?

    e. Which person would be easy to talk to? How could you tell?

    f. How would a rude person act? Did you see anyone in the story do that? Name other things that show rudeness.

g. If a person was impatient how would they act? Was anyone in the story impatient? Who? How did you know they weren't patient?

h. Did someone annoy people by talking too much or being too bossy? Who? How did others react?

i. How would someone act if they were being secretive? Why would they display those characteristics?

j. Was anyone trying to unravel a puzzle? How did you know? What steps did they take?

k. Did anyone in the story demonstrate they were unhappy? How did you know? What did they do to change their mood? Was that a good choice?

l. How would a gentle person act? Was there anyone in this story you would label gentle? What actions demonstrated that gentleness?

m. Did anyone give unwanted advice? How did others around him respond? Explain why they reacted that way.

ANSWER KEY FOR PURSUING GOLD

CHAPTER 1

1. What did Peter mean when he said C&R Bank was fully invested in the community?
   He put his money in community businesses and had nothing to spare.

2. Peter wanted bank dealings to be legal and fair. What type of man was he?
   He was a good man who wanted to do things right.

3. What is a rumor? Why would that frighten Mary Beth?
   She heard a story that spies might be coming to Chattanooga, and that scared her. During a war, city folk hear many rumors and have to decide which they should discount.

4. People did not have telephones in the 1860s. They sent messages by telegraph or mail instead.
   Look on the internet to see who invented phones.
   Alexander Graham Bell invented the phone in 1876.

5. What is the role of a spy?
   A spy gathers information on their enemies in order to bring about their defeat. Typically, a spy does not wear a uniform and the military hangs a spy when uncovered.

6. Could a Christian be a spy?
   Obviously, spies checked out Jericho before the invasion, and God blessed Rahab for choosing the side of the Israel. Anyone today who chooses to be a spy would have a lot of issues to consider.

7. Why was Chattanooga valuable to the Union?
   Railroads ran through Chattanooga, so Union Generals considered the city a key to gaining the South.

8. 'I wished I'm a never' was a saying common amongst country folk. What do you think it means?
   It means that's terrible.

CHAPTER 2

1. Based on what you see in the story, what do you think 'lying abed' means?
   The person was sick in bed.

2. Define prognosis.
   It means likely outcome.

3. Mr. Roper defined what a bank does. Share what he said.
   Why might a bank be important to the community?
   A banker uses the money deposited in the bank to invest in growing businesses in the community. The business that borrows pays back the money with interest. This helps businesses that need income to grow, and it also produces money for the bank so they can pay their employees.

4. What is a commodity?
   A commodity is an item considered valuable or necessary that people will pay for. Gold, silver, cotton, wheat can all be commodities.

5. What was a blockade?
   A blockade is a series of ships who attempt to close a harbor to trade. They might fire on the outgoing ships or take measures to sink any vessel trying to get in.

7. What did a blockade runner do?
   A blockade runner attempts to sneak by a blockade and carry on trade anyway.

8. What is a munitions factory and why would Peter hesitate to invest?
   A munitions factory makes ammunition like bullets or cannon balls.

9. Describe how you'd feel if you were stunned.
   A person who is stunned may have a hard time believing what they heard or saw. They might feel numb or feel surreal.

10. What did Eddie do that Mary Beth hated?
    Eddie flirted with other women and had a number of other girlfriends while he pursued Mary Beth.

CHAPTER 3

1. What do you think of Anna Chandler's plan?
   She wanted to distract people from the constant rumors, so they could attempt to live a normal life. In light of the situation, her idea was good. However, if troops had been nearby ready to invade, her plan would have been foolhardy. Seeking God's guidance on any decision is a good idea, since God knows the future.

2. You'll note that Mrs. Chandler refers to Ellen as Mrs. Reverend McCallie. That was common at the time. Why do you think they did that?

Using her husband's title associates her with her husband's job and sets her apart.

3. What did courtship mean in the 1860s?
A courting couple were considering marriage. The man would ask the father for permission to court the daughter.

4. Did it differ from today's dating?
Today dating is less serious.

5. What is foreshadowing?
It's an event that gives a glimpse of the future. The cat disliking Glass is foreshadowing.

6. Why would banking involve interacting with customers?
People like to do business with others they know and trust, especially those they meet at church. People tend to trust someone at church because they feel like they are honest. The practice can be dangerous these days because charlatans go to churches to get their prey.

7. Define trepidation.
Fear or anxiety.

8. What kind of man is Lieutenant McDonald?
How do you know?
He is not interested in Mary Beth's best interest. He is busy trying to flatter her to forward his own agenda.

9. 'Take the air' was another expression used at the time. What do you think it means?
It means to take a walk.

CHAPTER 4

1. Define dallied.
Put off responsibilities rather than get them out of the way.

2. What do you think of Ruth? Why?
Ruth appears distracted by soldiers and does not seem concerned for her mother. In this scene, she wants to escape the spilled coffee.

3. If you were Mrs. Chandler, how would you feel about an army targeting your town?
Answers will vary.

4. What impact did the telegraph have on communication?
It was expensive, but it was a great way to communicate. However, in the south, the telegraph did not always work.

5. What was the General?
The General was a train that ran between Big Shanty and Chattanooga.

6. What happened to it?

Northern spies stole it from the Big Shanty depot and tried to make it as far north as they could, destroying train lines as they went.

7. Describe Mr. Henderson.

Henderson is a politician consumed with his job. He cares about the community, but everything he says indicates he's thinking of his position and potential voters.

8. What is a clash of arms?

Fighting.

CHAPTER 5

1. Why didn't Mr. Nelson want Elsie in his store?

He did not like Elsie since she was a different color. Compare that attitude to Gal 3:28. The Bible says there are no longer divisions in Christ. In the church anyone who makes a profession of faith should be accepted (Of course, good judgment should be used to discern people's true characters, because there are charlatans in every church.)

2. What reason did Mr. Roper give for Mary Beth visiting the grocer?

Her father asked her to see how their business was doing.

3. How does that explain what a banker does?

As a banker, he wanted to offer help and advice to make them succeed since both would make money.

4. What two types of discrimination do we see in this chapter?

Discrimination of blacks and women. Both are prohibited in the New Testament.

5. Why doesn't God grant everything we pray for? See Isaiah 55:8–9

His thoughts are higher than ours. He is wiser because he knows the outcome of every choice we might make.

6. Mary Beth describes the problem of pain. If we believe God is good and all-powerful, why does he allow pain and suffering? Read Rom. 1: 18–32 and 8:28.

Scholars debate this question in seminaries, and C.S. Lewis describes it as the problem of pain, which only believers in Jesus have. From the verses listed, you can see God's punishment falls on everyone in the world because of our sin. However, he has the power to redeem even the most difficult situations. There's plenty of scope for discussion here.

CHAPTER 6

1. Dr. Smith tells Mary Beth her father is dying. Have you ever had someone close to you die? How did you feel?

Answer will vary.

2. Compare Mary Beth and Angela Phipps. Who do you like the best?
Angela Phipps is a typical martyr, while Mary Beth figures out how to get things done. Ask the students to think about what each of them has done to solve the problems they face and inch them through the topic. Mary Beth's father became ill, and she learned to care for him, even growing and preparing herbal tonics to help. Angela makes mistakes and cries, blaming someone else for everything.

3. What do you think of Gustav Sadler?
Some children struggle with this kind of question. If so, ask them to relate his actions and decide if they would like to be his friend.

4. What do you think of how Peter handled Sadler? Look at Matt. 5:23–25, Gal. 6:1, Matt. 18:15
Going to someone to talk about a something they've done wrong is what God asks us to do. We'd rather talk to anyone except the person who committed the error. Point out how Peter prepared beforehand with information from witnesses. He did not go angry.

5. Compare McDonald and Peter. Who do you like best?
McDonald is aggressive. Peter is polite, but careful what he agrees to do.

CHAPTER 7

1. What do Elsie's actions tell you about her?
Now that Mary Beth is grown, Elsie is working to become independent with her own sewing business. However, she offers to help Mary Beth on her time off. She also tends to scold like a mother. It's very obvious she loves Mary Beth.

2. Peter noted that everyone seemed to want the bank's money. Look up I Timothy 6:10, James 4:3 and tell why that's true.
It's easy for sinful people to lose their focus and seek after the wrong things. Money is a tool that can use for the kingdom but is not the answer to all our needs.

3. Why was Mary Beth angry with Peter when she found him talking to her father?
She feared Peter would bring stressful information from the bank. Any stress can injure a cardiac patient.

4. What risk did Peter take when he asked Mary Beth to consider courting him again?
He would be hurt if she refused. It's easy to get hurt when courting or dating. Peter went ahead because he'd promised Mr. Roper.

5. Would you have done what he did?

6. Why did Mary Beth respect Peter after he warned her about McDonald?
He wanted the best for her, even if it meant losing her.

CHAPTER 8

1. You'll notice Mary Beth weeding. Read Genesis 3:18 and explain why we have weeds.

   Genesis 3:18 said the ground would produce thorns and thistles after Adam and Eve's sin. God takes sin seriously, and we suffer the consequences.

2. How did Mary Beth know Ruth had something on her mind?

   Ruth seemed reluctant to talk and looked away.

3. What signals did Mr. Grant give that he was tense?

   He was shifting his weight back and forth, and he spoke hesitantly.

4. How dangerous would it be for Mr. Sadler to challenge Peter?

   Bank employees appeared to be worried Peter could not run the bank. Banking would be more difficult if they leave. Worse still, Sadler might attempt to undermine Peter's position.

CHAPTER 9

1. Fill in the blank using these words: infatuation, erupt, assignation, whim, scenario, pontificating

   A person who keeps talking so much others are annoyed is ***pontificating***

   Another name for a date is an ***assignation***.

   Erupt means a sudden gush.

   A sudden, crazy thought is a ***whim***.

   Feeling you might be in love is ***infatuation***.

2. Contrast Peter and Mary Beth's playtime.

   Peter planned meticulously down to the detail, making Mary Beth get bored and wander off.

3. When Mary Beth found her father in bed with bank papers, she tried to remove them, but he insisted on keeping them. Compare her thoughts with his.

   As a woman, Mary Beth was protective and nurturing. She grabbed the papers so her father would sleep. Her father was goal-oriented, and he wanted to finish going over the papers before he returned them to the bank.

4. At the end of the chapter, Mary Beth questions McDonald to learn more about him. What was his reaction?

   McDonald gave vague answers as if keeping her from knowing him.

5. What does this tell you about him?

   Being secretive could mean someone is not honest. When she continued to press him, he thought of something he had to do—an excuse to get away.

6. Sadler came to the Roper home and warned Mary Beth about Peter. How would you feel if someone talked negatively about someone you were coming to love?

Love and trust need to go together. This situation would be pretty intense, especially since Mary Beth trusted both Peter and Sadler all her life.

CHAPTER 10

1. Mary Beth goes to Peter and reports Sadler does not trust Peter's abilities. If you had been Peter, what would you do?

   The controversy here was between education and experience. Sadler had experience; Peter had education. Ideally, a banker should have both. However, Peter is truly more prepared than Sadler and can solve problems based on his education. Learning to think is so important in whatever we face, because we live in a damaged world and the worst sometimes happens.

2. What do you think of the way Sadler handled the situation?

   Sadler should have gone to Peter and shared his concerns rather than going behind his back.

3. In the 1860s people used coins of gold and silver rather than paper. People valued those metals. How would you feel if you were Mary Beth and found money counterfeited with your bank's name?

   As a banker's daughter, she would have been very upset. No one used paper because it was too easy to copy.

4. Describe the problem Mrs. Chandler had with Ruth.

   Ruth didn't want to go to Savannah and would not prepare to leave as her mother asked. Mrs. Chandler was discouraged and tried to talk Peter out of leaving.

5. Mrs. Chandler wants to solve Peter's problems. How much should she be involved?

   Mrs. Chandler made up her mind she would solve the problem with Sadler without telling Peter. Her son was an adult and her actions were not wise.

CHAPTER 11

1. Power of Attorney (POA) means you give someone permission to sign your name. Peter gave Mary Beth the ability to sign his name on bank documents while he was gone. How would you feel if someone gave you that permission?

   Have students share their emotions. Some kids may see a chance to be silly and convey large sums of money on themselves. The idea is to have them sense the responsibility.

2. Mary Beth discovers that her housekeeper, Maud, left without giving notice. Giving notice means you tell your employer you plan to stop working for him. Why do you think employers want 'notice'?

Employers would need to replace the employee. Notification gives them an opportunity to fill the vacancy quickly.

3. Note that the Roper's hired their servants. How is that different than a slave?
   A slave would not be able to leave, and the master could pursue the slave since he was considered the master's property.

4. What example do we have in Philemon regarding slaves and owners?
   In the book of Philemon, a slave named Onesimus escapes and even steals from Philemon, his employer. Later, Onesimus comes to Christ under the teaching of Paul the apostle. Paul feels compelled to send Onesimus back to Philemon, not as a slave, but as a beloved brother. This shows respect for Philemon but also shows respect for Onesimus because Paul asked Philemon to treat him as a brother, not a slave.

5. Mary Beth battles the problem of pain. As C.S. Lewis noted only Christians have the problem. We have a holy, all-powerful God, and yet he doesn't prevent suffering. In this chapter, she wonders if she should pray at all, because God doesn't seem to answer. What would you tell her?
   There are no easy answers, but we know God thinks in terms of eternity, not short-term like we do. He promises whatever happens to us, he can use it for good. We must believe that and rest in it.

6. Ruth pretends to be asleep because she doesn't want to be in Savannah. What do you think of such a tactic?
   It's not a mature way to deal with her problem. It's much better to be honest about what's bothering you. She is not respecting her mother but using manipulation to control the situation.

CHAPTER 12

Fill in the blank with the correct word: mimic, prospectus, lucrative, detest, dividends

1. If you hate something, you **detest** it.
2. When you want to borrow money, you write up a **prospectus** to convince the bank.
3. A business pays **dividends** to investors.
4. You **mimic** when you pretend to be someone else.

CHAPTER 13

1. How would you feel about going through someone's room looking for clues?
   Answers will vary.

2. Would you worry about being caught?

In the case of a crime being committed, police or detectives have to find clues. In this case, of course, Mary Beth and Peter were trying to keep their activities secret. A discussion can be held about personal boundaries.

3. Mary Beth and Mr. Grant worried how they would manage to work around Mr. Sadler. How did Mr. Grant do that?
Each time the bell rang, Mr. Sadler was alerted, so Mr. Grant took the bell down to clean it so Mary Beth could sneak in and get materials to investigate.

4. What do you think about his plan?
Answers will vary.

5. Peter prayed about every business he invested in. Why didn't he agree to invest in a factory that produced weapons?
He didn't want to be responsible for paying for munitions that might kill someone. He also would not invest in cotton clothing factories because they were closely associated with slave labor in the South.

6. Elsie stepped in the room while Mary Beth was paying bills. Why do you think Mary Beth was stressed?
As inflation grew, supplies were more expensive, and her father's salary was staying the same.

7. Does God care how we use our money? Read Luke 21:4, I Timothy 6:17.
Yes, he wants us to use it wisely and have eternal values.

8. Aunt Louise and Mrs. Chandler disagreed on how to handle Ruth. Who do you agree with?
Mrs. Chandler seemed to spoil Ruth, but Aunt Louise seemed to know Ruth's tricks. A good honest conversation with Ruth would have solved a lot of problems.

9. What indication did McDonald give Mary Beth that he didn't really care about her?
He was interested in what would happen to the bank if Mr. Roper died. Mary Beth wondered if he wanted the bank, not her.

CHAPTER 14

1. What indications do we have that Peter is becoming fond of Mary Beth?
    a. *He can't wait to see her when he arrives at the train station*
    b. *He has a hard time calculating the number of days he was gone.*
    c. *He wished he had brought a gift too.*
    d. *He looked forward to seeing her in the new dresses she would make.*

2. What do you think of how Peter handled the soldier who tried to start a fight?

He tried to avoid it, but when he was faced with defending himself, he pulled out his knife. Discuss why this was a good idea or a bad idea.

3. What hint do you get that telegrams might not always work?
   The telegram from Savannah did not reach Mary Beth.

4. How do you think Peter and Mary Beth's courtship is going?
   Their relationship is going well.

   a. *See number one.*
   b. *Mary Beth hurried to meet Peter.*
   c. *She pulled him into the house.*
   d. *Fluffing the hair around her face and talking about her new dresses.*

5. Why did Peter react when Mary Beth mentioned train accidents?
   His father was killed in a train accident.

6. Look up the word discrepancy and write the definition.
   An unacceptable difference.

Chapter 15

1. Explain why Peter was surprised to see Maud in his dining room.
   Maud was serving him, and she worked for Mary Beth.

2. Describe Maud.
   Maud is a talker. She has to say everything she thinks, and she talks so much she forgets the topic.

3. How does Maud describe McDonald? Do you agree?
   She believes he is evil. McDonald appears to be very much like Eddie, flirting to see what he can obtain for himself.

4. Why didn't Maud know to inform her employer before she left?
   As a former slave, she would not know about work etiquette.

5. What do you think of Mr. Roper's reaction to the news of counterfeit money?
   He knew it was serious, but he was confident of his own future. Plus, he expressed confidence that Peter could manage the bank even under such circumstances if he prayed for wisdom.

Chapter 16

1. If you were Mary Beth, would you have tried to avoid Ellen McCallie? Why?
   Sometimes people want to avoid others when they are depressed.

2. How do you feel about crying in public?
   Answers will vary. Make sure the student explains their answer.

3. Why do you think Peter shared his own troubles?
   He wanted Mary Beth to know about his own troubles and his need to trust in God. It's a good lesson for us all. Only God can meet our deepest needs.

4. Every banker fears a run on the bank. Describe what it is.
   A bank has to keep a certain amount of cash on hand. If everyone comes rushing to the bank to get their money at once, the bank will run out of money, and fail because they can't give everyone back their money.

5. What do you think about Peter asking Maud to work for Mary Beth as a spy?
   He was desperate to get Maud back to Mary Beth's, but the assignment might not have been the best approach.

CHAPTER 17

1. Maud found another counterfeit bill. Compare Maud's reaction to the bill to Mary Beth's reaction.
   Maud waited for Mary Beth and Peter to come home and handed it to them right away. She immediately blamed McDonald. Mary Beth felt guilty for not finding it with her cash. She examined it closely under the light.

2. How can you tell Bessie is tense?
   he was wringing her hands. When they asked her a question about the money, she widened her eyes.

3. Why did Peter question Bessie so closely?
   He wanted to know how the Ropers got the bill in hopes of finding the person who passed it.

4. How were Mary Beth and Peter different when they were alone at the bank?
   At first, they were all business but later they became playful.

CHAPTER 18

1. How do you think Mary Beth felt seeing McDonald after she expressed her deepest fear to Elsie?
   She would feel exposed, vulnerable, and might even wonder if McDonald heard her.

2. How would you have felt?
   *Answer may vary. (Note that Elsie didn't want McDonald to accompany Mary Beth alone. In that day, a young woman had escorts to protect her reputation. Being seen alone with a man could indicate she was courting him. In the light of the freedom we have today, we often scoff at such measures. However, being seen with someone of his reputation wouldn't be wise even today)*119

3. What rules does your family have in place to protect you?
   Answers will vary

4. What indication did McDonald give that he liked the comforts of life?
   He commented Negros were made for grueling labor, and he expressed a desire to be a business man or even a plantation owner. Possibly he had no idea how hard a plantation owner or businessman worked.

5. Mary Beth unearthed pictures and mementos in her father's desk. How would that make you feel knowing you would soon lose a parent?
   Answers will vary.

6. How important is it for the person who forged the money knew Peter ran the bank?
   Very important. The person must know the value of Peter's signature.

CHAPTER 19

1. Who cared for Mary Beth's father while she attended the party?
   Mrs. Haskell volunteered to sit with him.

2. Why did they have the party?
   Jane Haskell missed Mary Beth's tea party, and her parents wanted to make up for Jane's absence.

3. Contrast Peter and Mrs. Black.
   Mrs. Black takes over the party games and convinces everyone to participate. She enjoys people and lively games. On the other hand, Peter would rather be reading a book.

4. What do you learn about Mrs. Chandler in this chapter?
   She is determined to support Peter, and she will do anything in her power to protect him.

5. What was Mr. Sadler doing when Mrs. Chandler came in?
   He was working on bank ledgers.

6. Why did Mr. Sadler back down?
   Mrs. Chandler reminded him of her loyalty to his wife and his commitment to their family.

CHAPTER 20

1. Read the following verses and talk about what life changes you can make to avoid anxiety. Phil 4:6–9

   a. *Pray rather than being anxious*

   b. *Pray with thanksgiving, praising God for the answer.*

      i. *God promises to garrison about your mind with peace when you pray.*

      ii. *Think about things that are good, excellent, and praiseworthy.*

      iii. *Your thoughts cause/impact your emotions.*

2. Why is death so jarring? Read Genesis 2:16
   It's not natural. We all have a desire to continue living.

3. Have you ever lost a family member? How did you feel?
   This is a sensitive topic for some children. Answers will vary and some students may wish not to answer.

4. Mary Beth and Peter were both shocked by the sudden death of Sadler. Is grieving wrong?
   I Thess. 4:13. Psalm 88. Grieving is not wrong, and it's important to allow ourselves to go through the grieving process.

5. Now that Sadler is dead, what problem do Mary Beth and Peter have?
   They have no suspect.

CHAPTER 21

1. Find the definition of betray in the dictionary.
   Betray is to disappoint expectations of a friend or demonstrate disloyalty.

2. How would you feel if someone you trusted betrayed you?
   It hurts. You wish you had never trusted that person.

3. Read Ps 55, especially verses 12 to 21. What happened to David?
   David's friend betrayed his trust.

4. A metaphor is comparing two items without the use of like or as. What metaphor/metaphors does David use in verse 21 to describe his former friend?
   Speech compared to smooth butter/words soothing like oil; Words compared to war and drawn swords

5. Why did Peter need to interview bank employees? *Sadler had been stealing money, and Peter also suspected he might be in the counterfeiting scheme. Now his only suspect died, he needs to find out what the others know.*

6. What is foreshadowing?
   Giving a hint of what will happen later.

7. What's an example in this chapter of foreshadowing?
   Peter saw the coat on the coat tree and wondered why it wasn't put away.

8. What's behind Mary Beth's suspicion of Mrs. Phipps?
   Mrs. Phipps acted oddly, and Mary Beth wondered if Angela Phipps had romantic intentions toward Peter.

CHAPTER 22

1. Why would a cup of tea with sugar be refreshing?
   Stress causes the throat to dry and the warm tea would feel good. (The teacher can add: Peter is facing a stressful situation, and the sugar would give extra energy.)

2. Why do you think Mary Beth was no longer itching to get home to her father?
   Maud agreed to look after her father. Peter appears stressed and overloaded, and she is falling in love with Peter.

3. Describe Mrs. Sadler. How is she different than Mary Beth?
   Mrs. Sadler is crippled, opinionated, and proud. Mary Beth is compassionate but not sure of herself.

4. What do you think of them sedating Mrs. Sadler?
   Answers will vary.

5. How does Mrs. Chandler react when she hears Sadler is dead?
   Shock. She almost blurts out she just saw him, but that would reveal her secret.

6. What gift did Sadler give the Chandler family?
   He gave them his diaries.

CHAPTER 23

1. Why was Sadler's funeral dreary?
   The lack of sun emphasized how Sadler's character had changed.

2. Was it just the lack of sunlight?
   Once he could be trusted, but he turned to embezzlement and maybe counterfeiting.

3. Why couldn't Peter share the entire truth with the congregation at Sadler's funeral?
   He wanted to respect the grieving family.

4. Why did Peter have the dream about his father?
The dream had come off and on as he grieved his father's death. Given the problems at the bank, he felt like he was failing his father.

5. What new rules might Peter put in place to protect the bank?
He might control access to the upstairs or maybe even lock certain items in the bank office. He could also restrict who had keys to the door.

6. Why did Mary Beth suddenly agree to take Sadler's place?
She had time to think how she could work around her father's care, and she did work faster than Sadler. Maud agreed to help with her father's care also.

7. What explanation did Dr. Smith give for Sadler's need for extra income?
is mother had health issues, which meant she needed someone to care for her. Hiring Miss Fitch was putting pressure on their budget.

8. Both Peter and Mary Beth wanted to know if Sadler's death could be murder. Explain the doctor's answer.
Sadler broke his neck after a fall down the stairs. Dr. Smith could not be sure what caused the fall. Perhaps Mr. Sadler's arthritis was bothering him, or perhaps he was pushed.

CHAPTER 24

1. What do you think about Sheriff Campbell?
Answers will vary.

2. What plan did Mary Beth have to determine how many counterfeit bills might be circulating?
She asked her friends to look for the bills, pretending she loved the artwork.

3. What did Fanny have on her mind?
Flirting with soldiers.

4. Which of the girls seemed the most reasonable?
Ida and Jane.

5. Why didn't Anna keep her midnight visit from Sheriff Campbell?
The sheriff already had witnesses who saw her, and she didn't want to be accused of murder.

6. How are Sargent Glass and Peter different?
Sargent Glass is rude, selfish, and disrespectful. Peter is gracious and rational. Even though he's a young man, he can be firm if he has to be.

CHAPTER 25

1. Compare Mary Beth and Peter's relationship in this chapter to the first part of the book.

    In the beginning, they were friends, but they didn't communicate well. Mary Beth resented Peter's tendency to get the facts. In the later part of the story, you can see them starting to work together and enjoy each other.

2. Why did Peter agree to allow Mary Beth to interview Mrs. Fuller?

    The family was poor, and Mrs. Fuller was already intimidated by people from the bank. Mary Beth was less frightening.

3. Why did Mrs. Fuller appear afraid when Mary Beth mentioned money?

    hey had little money, and Mrs. Fuller might worry about a debt her husband had not paid. Mary Beth had always been intimidated by Reverend McCallie's long face and deep-set eyes.

4. Why shouldn't a person base their opinion only on how someone looks?

    Answers will vary.

5. Did Mary Beth's fear prove to be valid? Explain.

    No. McCallie was very kind and allowed her to talk.

6. How did McCallie help Mary Beth?

    He didn't condemn her for her emotional reaction to her father's upcoming death. Instead he told her we can't always see what God is doing because of our own pain. He advised her to read Ps. 88 to show how grieving is acceptable.

CHAPTER 26

1. How did Anna's mood change when she got the anonymous letter?

    She went from being excited about having Mary Beth over to being horrified she might cause her son's death. Plus, she didn't have a chance to calm down before Mary Beth arrived.

2. How would you have responded?

    Answers will vary.

3. Mary Beth admitted to feeling guilt when she was away from her father and enjoying herself. Why do you think she felt that way?

    Caregivers feel so responsible they can't enjoy themselves when someone else cares for the sick person. Rest is important for physical, spiritual, and emotional health. (The teacher can add: This is a common problem for caregivers.)

4. Mary Beth took charge of the situation when she and Mrs. Chandler found the mess in the library. Why didn't Mrs. Chandler take a more active role?
She was probably still thinking about the note she received, and she hadn't had experience solving puzzles like Mary Beth.

5. Why did Peter think of Ruth when he saw the office disaster?
He would never accuse his mother or the servants. She was the only one who might know what happened.

6. How did Mary Beth know Ruth was holding back?
Ruth was looking away, not making eye contact, and even edging toward Mary Beth.

CHAPTER 27

1. What do you think of Peter and Mary Beth's plan to search for counterfeit money?
It was a wonderful idea because as bankers they got to interact with their customers to find out how things were going, and their plan gave Mary Beth to see what kind of money they had in their possession.

2. What did Mary Beth do when she found a forged bill?
She added it into the quarterly interest payment they needed to make.

3. Why was this a good solution?
It was a great idea because she didn't have to announce the reason she wanted the bill.

4. When the printer asked Mary Beth if she was ready to print her calling cards, how did she answer?
(Girls often had calling cards at that time, especially wealthy people.) She said her name might change, which was true because she and Peter were considering marriage.

5. Mary Beth finally speaks to Dr. Bell about Glass, which shows growth in her personality. She would have never done that when the story began. What do you think about Bell's reaction?
Bell made excuses for Glass, which wasn't very wise. People should experience the consequences of their behavior.

6. How could the state of Tennessee solve Peter's problem?
Dr. Smith reported the Union passed a bill saying that no one could go to the bank and demand gold for the dollars. The paper money merely represented gold and most bills said you could exchange the paper for gold. Peter's concern was that clients would come to the bank with counterfeit bills and demand gold. If too many came at once the bank

would fail. However, if Tennessee passed a law like the Union, the problem would be solved.

CHAPTER 28

1. Notice Mr. Roper's comment that Sadler was secretive. Read John 3:19–20 and explain why.
   When you are in darkness and light comes along it hurts your eyes. The same is true for someone living in sin and appearing secretive. They do not want to be around the light because it reveals their sin.

2. How can the information you learned about secretive people impact how your life?
   Remember people are sinners and might not be trustworthy. Make wise judgments about who you trust. Trust is like a bridge it takes a long time to build, one brick at a time over time.

3. How did Mary Beth respond to the medical emergency with her father? Why?
   She became worried and said she couldn't face it. Based on what she said in the past, we know she doesn't want to be an orphan. (Some people feel like an orphan when their parents die even as an adult.) She was now facing her greatest fears, and that's a tough position.

4. Mary Beth worried about the bank. How does Peter answer?
   He said the bank could wait. Do you agree with his decision to stay with Mary Beth? Why or why not?
   Answers will vary.

5. A vigil like this can be very difficult for the family. How did Peter and Mary Beth cope?
   They drank hot tea and chatted. Today psychologist realize emotions are best processed with others.
   What does their relationship look like?
   Peter was very supportive of Mary Beth.

6. How does sleep impact your health?
   Lack of sleep increases levels of cortisol circulating in your blood. Continual high levels reduce immunity, make you more prone to diabetes, high blood pressure, high blood sugar, and resistance to insulin. It's important to learn your diurnal rhythm, maintaining a good balance of rest, diet, exercise, and sleep.

7. Compare Mary Beth's reaction to the bombing and Reverend McCallie's.
   The minister kept praying right through the bombing. Mary Beth sank onto the floor. She tried to pray, but all she could get out was, "Help."

CHAPTER 29

1. Has Mary Beth's faith improved? If so, how?
   She has decided to believe even though she doesn't fully understand.

2. Hearing is the last sense to leave the body. So, caregivers should be careful what they say even when the patient is unresponsive. What does Mary Beth say to her father?
   "I love you."

3. Have you ever noticed people whisper when they talk about death?
   Answers will vary.

4. The conversation Peter and Mary Beth have at Roper's bedside is intense. What would you be feeling if you were Mary Beth?
   ad, broken-hearted.

5. Peter joined Mary Beth as her father is slipping away. What did Peter say when Mary Beth mentions the bank?
   "Banking can wait."

6. Do you agree?
   Answers will vary.

7. Mary Beth felt alone and believed no one cared after the funeral. Was she accurate?
   *Mary Beth wasn't alone even though she felt alone. That is very common when someone suffers great trauma. If you read C. S. Lewis's book **A Grief Observed**, you can see how alone he felt after his wife died.*

8. How might her thoughts reflect grieving? See Ps. 88.
   She was not alone, and yes, people cared. Mary Beth was grieving. The passage in Psalms reflects the thoughts of a depressed person, and the psalm does not resolve at the end like most psalms.

9. How did Peter's priorities change at the end of the chapter?
   The bank had been his highest priority until this point. Now Mary Beth is the most important.

CHAPTER 30

1. Why couldn't Mary Beth sleep at the Chandler home?
   She couldn't fully relax.

2. Describe the young man Mary Beth saw.
   He was small, wiry. He said one word at a time and never made eye contact.

3. Why do you think Ruth left a message in the woods? Explain.
   She probably wanted John to know she would return.

4. Mary Beth wasn't happy Peter sent Maud to spy on Mary Beth. How would you feel if someone spied on you?
   It might make me question their loyalty.

5. Why does Ruth speak more easily with Mary Beth?
   She doesn't feel comfortable talking to her mother. There's no baggage with Mary Beth.

6. Can you guess who the midnight visitor is?
   John. (Some students may have a different answer. Discuss how the conclusion was reached.)

CHAPTER 31

1. How did Mary Beth find comfort the next morning?
   She found a Bible by the bed and read verses about Jesus Mrs. Chandler had marked.

2. Contrast how Mary Beth felt about her mother and how Ruth felt about hers.
   Mary Beth longed for her mother. She would gaze at photos and wonder what she was like. Ruth felt misunderstood and didn't think her mother cared. She wished she didn't have a mother.

3. Why was Peter dismayed by Mary Beth's announcement?
   He didn't want Mary Beth working at the hospital because he was concerned for her safety. Plus, he didn't think she would learn anything useful.

4. How do you think Mary Beth will investigate at the hospital?
   She will have to sneak around. With so many patients that will be hard.

CHAPTER 32

1. Do you think Peter will obey Sheriff Campbell and stop snooping?
   No, although Mary Beth was the one he worried about.

2. Why did Mary Beth react so strongly to her first patient's death?
   She was still grieving her father's death.

3. Why do you think Mary Beth was drawn to Major General Connelly?
   He was gracious and was about the age of her father.

4. Do you think Peter's concerns for Mary Beth's safety are realistic? Why or why not?

Answers will vary. Remember the soldier who attacked Peter for almost no reason. Very young soldiers don't always make the best choices.

CHAPTER 33

1. What did Mary Beth learn as she perused the unused portion of Newsome Hospital?

It was filled with woodworking tools but no counterfeit money.

2. What regrets did Connelly have?

He wouldn't be in active duty anymore, and his daughter was too busy to spend time with him.

3. Why did McDonald turn nasty and shoot at Peter?

He was drunk, which lowered his inhibitions.

4. What puzzle did Peter solve in his library?

He found a letter with his signature missing, and he knew that's where the forged signature came from.

CHAPTER 34

1. Why didn't Peter report McDonald earlier?

hey were still looking for the counterfeiting culprit. Once McDonald attacked him, he knew he'd best report him.

2. Why was Mary Beth reluctant to share with Connelly?

She didn't want to burden him and delay his recovery.

3. What did Mary Beth learn from Connelly?

He told her about the story of Daniel, who had to leave his home at an early age. He wanted his people to be back in Israel worshipping God, but that wouldn't happen in his lifetime. God showed Daniel the future when his dream would come true.

4. How did that change her perspective?

Mary Beth realized what God had provided in her grief, and she learned to think long term. For instance, Ruth and Naomi didn't realize how God would use their pain. Ruth's baby became part of the genealogy of Christ, something she could never have anticipated.

5. How can the same truth impact your life?
   When bad things happen and dreams fall apart, we should still seek God like we pursue Gold. God honors you if your desires are holy.

CHAPTER 35

1. How did Peter and Mary Beth feel when they found the counterfeit money?
   Elated, shocked.

2. Why did George Bell kill Mr. Allen?
   He was demanding money, and Bell didn't want to give him any.

3. How did they find out George Bell was the counterfeiter?
   Bell admitted it when he saw the money exposed.

4. How Connelly know Mary Beth needed help?
   Connelly saw her enter the room with a man, and then he heard a ruckus.

CHAPTER 36

1. Why did Mrs. Chandler have stomach problems?
   An upset stomach can result from stress.

2. Do you think she regretted her secretive actions that brought the sheriff to visit?
   She was terrified she would be charged with Sadler's murder. If she had known the outcome of her midnight visit to the bank, she might have chosen a different plan to make Sadler relent.

3. Tell what happened after she took her burdens to God.
   She resolved the problem with Ruth.

4. Why would Peter hide his pain from Mary Beth?
   She had fainted from the stress of the attack, and he didn't want to burden her until he knew she was well.

5. Is this the same as Mrs. Chandler hiding her actions regarding Sadler?
   No.

6. Why or why not?
   (Answers may vary.) Mrs. Chandler intended to keep the secret all the way to her grave.

7. Who was George Bell and why was he important?
   George Bell's father had married Mrs. Chandler's mother after her own father died. George wanted to get even with Andrew Chandler, because Andrew did not accept

George's father as a bank partner. He was the doctor who was staying in Mary Beth's home.

8. Who was Ruth's new friend?
John was a boy younger than Ruth who had no friends.

9. How did that friendship explain her hesitancy to go to Savannah?
She wanted to help him since he did not seem to fit in anywhere.

10. Who took Peter's signature off the letter?
Ruth had allowed John access to the office. He tore the signature off a letter because his father convinced him to. John had no idea what his father would use it for.

11. How did the cotton convince Mary Beth to look further for the culprit?
Nothing she saw in the bank explained the cotton, and she believed it had to do with the use of chloroform. She was correct.

BIBLIOGRAPHY

Ackerman, Angela and Puglisi, Becca, *The Emotion Thesaurus: A Writers Guide to Character Expression*, Amazon Digital Publishing, 2019

Derks, Scott, *The Value of a Dollar: Prices and Income in the United States, 1860–2004*, Grey House Publishing, Millerton, NY, 2004

Friedberg, Arthur and Friedberg, Ira, *A Guide Book of United States Paper Money: Complete Source for History, Grading, and Value*, Fourth Edition, Whitman Publishing, 2019

Friedberg, Robert, *Paper Money of the United States: A Complete and Illustrated Guide with Valuations*, Second Edition, The Coin and Currency Publishing Institute, New York, 1955

Gilden, Linda, and Goldfarb, Linda, *Linked: Maximizing Life Connections One Link at a Time*, Bold Vision Books, 2018

Mihm, Stephen, *A Nation of Counterfeiters: Capitalists, Con Men, and the Making of the United States*, Harvard University Press, 2007

Sources for Socratic Questions:

https://en.wikipedia.org/wiki/Socratic_questioning

http://www.umich.edu/~elements/probsolv/strategy/cthinking.htm

https://www.opencolleges.edu.au/informed/features/socratic-questioning/

Schwab, John Christopher, A.M, Ph.D., *The confederate States of America 1861–1865, A Financial and Industrial History of the South During the Civil War*, Yale Bicentennial Publications, Charles Scribner and Sons, New York, London, Edward Arnold. 1901, Reprinted by Astrologic Books, New York, 2007

Temperaments: Accessed May 2019

https://www.google.com/search?newwindow=1&sa=G&hl=en&q=4+temperaments+test&tbm=isch&tbs=simg:CAQSkwEJrzjAh52ORYcahwELEKjU2AQa-AAwLELC

Made in the USA
Columbia, SC
25 September 2019